NEBUCHADNEZZAR

Is After My Child

by:

Terry G. Gooding

© 2017 Terry G. Gooding. All Rights Reserved. Unauthorized Duplication is Prohibited.

Copyright © 2017 Terry G. Gooding. United States of America. All Rights Reserved under international copyright laws. Contents and/or cover may not be reproduced in whole or in part without prior written consent.

Printed in the United States of America

Published by Aion Multimedia
20118 N 67th Ave
Suite 300-446
Glendale AZ 85308
www.aionmultimedia.com

ISBN-13: 978-0-9976046-6-5

Scripture quotations marked (KJV) are taken from the King James Bible, New York: American Bible Society: 1999.

Table of Contents

Preface
Introduction
Part I - The Thief Cometh To Steal!

Chapter 1 - The Satanic Conspiracy   11
Chapter 2 - To Kidnap And To Conquer   17
Chapter 3 - The Fight For Control   23
Chapter 4 - What Kind Of Attitude Is This?   33
Chapter 5 - Satan Wants To Get 'Em In Their Prime   41
Chapter 6 - Teach Your Children Well   45
Chapter 7 - How Far Do We Go?   53
Chapter 8 - Change Their Nature   59

Part II - The Thief Cometh To Kill!

Chapter 9 - Satan Wants To Kill Your Dreams   65
Chapter 10 - Who Is Your God?   71
Chapter 11 - Do I Know You?   75
Chapter 12 - You Are What You Eat   83
Chapter 13 - The devil IS Making Them do it!   87

Part III - The Thief Cometh To Destroy!

Chapter 14 - Satan's Tentacles Have Stretched Into The New Millennium   99
Chapter 15 - But I Don't Like My Name   107
Chapter 16 - Mpingo Jua, Hananiah, Mishael, Azariah and Daniel   111
Chapter 17 - Parents Have To Go To War!   121

Part IV - I Am Come That You Might Have Life

Chapter 18 - Youth Have Got To Be SMART   133
Chapter 19 - You've Got To Be Single-Minded   137
Chapter 20 - You've Got To Be Alert   147
Chapter 21 - You've Got To Be Resolute   165
Chapter 22 - You've Got To Be Tenacious   169

Part V - . . . And That You Might Have It (Life) More Abundantly

Chapter 23 - Remember NOW Thy Creator   175
Chapter 24 - God Is Calling   185
Conclusion: Be About Your Father's Business   193

Acknowledgements

To my children, Cheri, Faithon and Terrance,
who made me learn how to be a Christian parent

* * *

To my mother, Annie Pearl Gooding,
who made me go to Sunday School
and prayed without ceasing for me
when I thought I was too grown to go anymore

* * *

To my wife, Eunice, for your love, patience, support
and understanding during the many hours
I spent developing this work

Preface

Train up a child in the way he should go, and when he is old, he will not depart from it. - Proverbs 22:6

Our youth are under attack. They are being deluged by a myriad of challenges that threaten their futures. These challenges are being orchestrated by satan who is stalking them like a roaring lion seeking to devour their lives on earth and their eternal souls. Yes, while many people in today's modern world don't believe in a "devil" as described in the Bible, he is very real and is like a renegade on the loose.

The purpose of this book is to expose the strategy satan is using to destroy our youth and where that strategy originated, as well as to provide counter-measures youth can use to defeat him. It's also intended to help parents help their children successfully navigate through the perilous times of their youth.

This is a unique book. It's primarily targeted toward parents who love their children, want the best for them, but are often frustrated and perplexed by their attitudes and actions. It's also a resource for youth, particularly those who have been reared in a Christian environment, to use as a guide to navigate through the complications of teenage and early adult life. But, it's also pertinent to any believer in Christ who wants to understand the tactics satan uses in his untiring attempt to prevent people from connecting with God.

The book provides tools and resources to help parents and youth withstand the onslaught of the devil. It's based on research, personal parental experience and many years of working with youth ministerially and professionally. The research provides the sobering picture of the toll satan is taking on our youth. The personal experience provides practical and humorous vignettes about how I as a parent waged the battle to protect my children from becoming victims.

Parenting is a great responsibility and perhaps the most difficult job anyone can have. If you're currently raising children or have raised children, you'll relate to and appreciate the content and stories in this book. But beware; from time-to-time you're likely to find yourself staring from the pages based on parenting experiences you've had.

Oh, one last thing. I'm an old guy so forgive me for using some old-school references. I trust some readers will be in my age category and appreciate the trivia. And, if you're in the younger crowd, I believe you'll enjoy the history.

Introduction

I believe this book can be one of the most important tools a parent can have in their child-rearing toolbox during these perilous end times. However, there is something I must establish at the outset.

I'm going to talk explicitly about satan, or the devil, and the fact that he is real and not just a figment of our imagination or a slick creation of hollywood movie producers. If you don't believe satan is real, this book won't have the impact that it could for you. It will simply become just another document containing some usable information you may refer to from time to time, depending on the circumstances.

On the other hand, if you believe satan does in fact exist, as the Bible unequivocally declares, then you'll completely understand the rationale behind the book and how the premise is based on his diabolical and destructive nature. You'll also, in turn, fully understand his relentless onslaught on the youth of our world and how he will not stop until he drags as many of them as possible to hell with him.

But let me be clear. This is not about giving glory to satan. It's about exposing him for what he is—a ruthless, wicked, fallen angel whose sole goal is to destroy mankind in a perverted attempt to try to get back at God.

This is about making sure people, primarily our precious young people, are fully informed about the enemy of their souls.

Who and what is satan?

The American Heritage Dictionary defines satan as "in some religions, the major spirit of evil and foe of God; a subordinate evil spirit; a wicked or malevolent person; to annoy, torment or attack."

If you're not familiar with the term "malevolent" it's synonymous with malicious, spiteful, wicked, nasty and means having or showing a desire to harm others.

Obviously, the publishers of dictionaries aren't necessarily viewing things from spiritual eyes. But in this case, the authors of the American Heritage Dictionary did a great job of describing the foe that everyone on planet earth has to contend with daily.

That's because the American Heritage authors give a description of satan that's very similar to the description contained in the Bible–particularly from the standpoint that he is the primary "foe" and enemy of God.

From a Biblical point of view, I like the description provided by The New Compact Bible Dictionary. It describes satan as a common noun "enemy or adversary"; and as a proper noun, "the chief of the fallen spirits, the grand adversary of God and man hostile to everything good".

It's important here to emphasize the last part of that definition "hostile to everything that is good". Being hostile or opposed to everything that is good means that satan endorses or approves everything that is bad.

This notion is born out in the various Biblical descriptive designations given to satan. These designations, as well as the Biblical passages where they can be found in the King James version of the Bible, are listed below:

- devil (Matthew 4:1)
- the tempter (Matthew. 4:5)
- beelzebub devil or prince of devils (Matthew 12:24)
- the evil one (Matthew 13:19)
- the father of lies (John 8:44)
- murderer (John 8:44)
- the god of this world (II Corinthians 4:4)
- the prince of the powers of the air (Ephesians 2:2)
- accuser of the brethren (Revelation 12:9)
- deceiver of the whole world (Revelation 12:9)
- the great dragon (Revelation 12:9)
- the old serpent (Revelation12:9)

Common Christian vernacular refers to satan as the devil. The New Compact Bible Dictionary interprets the devil as "slanderer, one of the principal titles of satan, the arch-enemy of God and man."

Believe it or not, satan actually was an angel named Lucifer, created by God. He was not created evil. But he was lifted up in pride and decided he wanted to take control of Heaven or elevate himself above God. He consequently led other angels into rebellion in Heaven. In response, God

Introduction

cast him and his minions (a third of the angels) out of Heaven and onto planet earth.

At least two accounts of satan's fall are recorded in the Bible, one in Isaiah chapter 14 verses 12 through14. *"How art thou fallen from heaven, O Lucifer, son of the morning! How art thou cut down to the ground, which didst weaken the nations!*

"For thou hast said in thine heart, I will ascend into heaven, I will exalt my throne above the stars of God; I will sit also upon the mount of the congregation, in the sides of the north;

"I will ascend above the heights of the clouds: I will be like the most High".

Another account is found in Ezekiel 28:14-17: *"Thou art the anointed cherub that covereth; and I have set thee so; thou wast upon the holy mountain of God; thou hast walked up and down in the midst of the stones of fire.*

"Thou wast perfect in thy ways from the day that thou wast created, till iniquity was found in thee.

"By the multitude of thy merchandise they have filled the midst of thee with violence, and thou hast sinned; therefore I will cast thee as profane out of the mountain of God: and I will destroy thee, O covering cherub, from the midst of the stones of fire.

"Thine heart was lifted up because of thy beauty, thou hast corrupted thy wisdom by reason of thy brightness: I will cast thee to the ground, I will lay thee before kings, that they may behold thee."

The unfortunate problem for all of us is that when satan was cast onto planet earth he brought his hordes or followers to earth with him to take revenge out on God by targeting mankind.

This obviously puts us in a perilous position. It means we have to live in a world that is ruled by the most ruthless being ever created by God. Adolph Hitler, the leader of the Nazi (Nationalist Socialist German Workers) Party, who attempted to create a supreme race of people by ordering the execution of approximately six million European Jews, couldn't hold a candle to satan's ruthlessness. If fact, Hitler was only a pawn that satan used to take the natural lives of God's chosen people.

God's Word further describes satan as *"the prince and the power of the air, the spirit that now worketh in the children of disobedience"*. (Ephesians 2:22)

After he landed on earth, since he couldn't overcome God in Heaven, his one overwhelming purpose would be to destroy the children of men. That's why John said in his writing that *"the thief (satan) cometh not but for to steal, kill and to destroy"*. (St. John 10:10a)

If you can't destroy the maker, why not go after the ones the maker made? And that's exactly what he's done.

During the course of time, satan has attacked kings. He's attacked prophets. He's attacked preachers. He's attacked the weak and the strong. He's attacked the educated, and the uneducated. He's attacked the sick and the well, including those with mental and physical disability.

His relentless attack on the human race started way back in the Garden of Eden. The book of Genesis chapter three, verse one gives the account.

"Now the serpent (possessed by satan) was more subtil than any beast of the field which the Lord God had made. And he said unto the woman, Yea, hath God said, Ye shall not eat of every tree of the garden." (Genesis 3:1)

It's necessary to understand a couple of things about what the scripture says here. First, it says the serpent was *"more subtil (cunning) than any beast of the field"*. We have to recognize that satan is shrewd, he's crafty, and he's deceitful. He has no equal when it comes to playing mind games for the purpose of making you believe a lie.

Secondly, it's vital to understand that satan will talk to you—"*And he said unto the woman.*" He'll talk to your mind. He'll talk to your heart. He'll talk to your spirit. He has the ability to speak so smoothly he can make you believe what he says. He is very articulate. He knows how to use the right words at the right time to influence a person to accept his perverted, ungodly views.

The reason it is critical that Christians know the Word of God for themselves is because satan will take the very words of God and twist them in a way to use to his advantage. Notice that satan said, "*Yea, hath God said, Ye shall not eat of every tree of the garden*"; when in actuality

Introduction

God said for them not to eat of but one tree. *"But of the tree of the knowledge of good and evil, thou shalt not eat of it."* (Genesis 2:17)

In this regard, satan is the ultimate con artist, the ultimate sweet talker, who can virtually talk a baby into handing over his candy.

That's why it's emphasized in Ephesians chapter 6, verses 11 and 12 for us to *"Put on the whole armor of God, that ye may be able to stand against the wiles (devious or cunning actions used to manipulate) of the devil. For we wrestle not against flesh and blood, but against principalities, against powers, against rulers of the darkness of this world, against spiritual wickedness in high places (the mind)."*

The combination of satan's ability to deceive and smooth-talk people allowed him to beguile Eve into accepting his lie. It caused her to disbelieve what God had said and then convince Adam to eat from the one tree—the tree of the knowledge of good and evil—that God said they couldn't eat from. And that one surrender to temptation plummeted all of humanity into the bondage of sin.

All Christians must thoroughly understand that the chief weapon satan uses is deceit. That's why Jesus was emphatic in Mathew 24:3 when responding to the disciples' questions about the end times.

"And as he sat upon the Mount of Olives, the disciples came unto him privately, saying tell us, when shall these things be? And what shall be the sign of thy coming, and of the end of the world?"

Jesus firmly declared *"take heed that no man deceive you!"* *(Exclamation point added)*

The devil is so confident in his ability to twist the Word of God around to deceive people that he even attacked Jesus. Make no mistake about it. Satan's evil nature has no boundaries. He'll go after anything and anybody.

Imagine satan's boldness when he tempted Jesus in the wilderness. Mathew chapter eight, verse four says *"Again, the devil taketh him up into an exceeding high mountain, and sheweth him all the kingdoms of the world, and the glory of them; and saith unto him (Jesus), all these things will I give thee, if thou wilt fall down and worship me."*

This particular scripture vividly describes several elements satan uses to tempt the people of God: *"the kingdoms of the world"* and the *"glory of them"*. The kingdoms of the world relate to the power or authority that men want and the glory of them relate to man's pride or egotism about what he has or owns.

I John 2:16 explains this another way. It says all that is in the world is the lust of the flesh (our natural or fleshly desires), the lust of the eye (the things we want that we see) and the pride of life (things that feed our ego).

He's after our children

Satan will use and is using all these tools of temptation and more to bring down mankind. But perhaps the most ruthless attack he has unleashed yet is upon our children.

His attack upon our children has escalated dramatically and tragically during the last 30 years, but it didn't just begin 30 years ago. It's an attack he launched way back in the book of Genesis when Cain got upset with his brother Abel and took his life.

The story is found in Genesis chapter 4, versus 1 through 12. The murder is recorded in verse 8: *"And Cain talked with Abel his brother, and it came to pass, when they were in the field, that Cain rose up against Abel his brother, and slew him"*.

Another clear example of satan's conspiracy to destroy youth is the story about Joseph and how his brothers decided they'd had enough of their younger brother's "foolish" dreams and decided to get rid of him. (Genesis 37:19&20) We'll examine this in detail later.

As a result of satan's all-out attack, the youth of our world is in crisis. Young people are dying in great numbers. Others are behind bars in juvenile detention centers. Many others are being ravaged by drugs, alcohol, sexually transmitted diseases, violence, suicide and many other maladies satan is using to destroy them.

Many parents are in full-out panic mode, unsure and confused about how to best guide and protect their children, particularly from a Christian standpoint. As the world has grown increasingly liberal, the parenting principles, morals and values which used to be widely accepted and held dear, are no longer acceptable by society at large.

Psychologists, sociologists and community leaders tend to pin the blame on prominent societal problems such as the issues of latchkey kids,

Introduction

fathers who are missing in action, single parent households, violence in the media, violent rap lyrics and a blatant disregard for authority.

While these are all contributing factors which I'll discuss throughout this book, I contend there is a much deeper, more devilish reason we're losing so many of our young people.

The deeper root cause

Nebuchadnezzar Is After My Child proposes that the root cause goes back to what many in our society are dismissing as outdated and irrelevant in today's modern world—and that is God and the principles for living that are contained in His Word—the Holy Bible. Consequently, I believe the ultimate cause of a lost generation is the loss of a belief and consciousness that God exists.

And the book goes one step future. It explains in plain terms that this loss of God consciousness in our world among youth can fundamentally be attributed to the ferocious unleashing of a satanic influence on our world that can be traced back to Babylon where King Nebuchadnezzar in vivid detail shows us the strategy of the devil to destroy young people.

The story of Nebuchadnezzar shows us that what's happening in our society today has been a conspiracy all along, a conspiracy by satan to steal our children, not only from us parents, but ultimately from God.

Part I

The Thief Cometh To Steal!

Chapter 1

The Satanic Conspiracy

"The thief cometh not, but for to steal, to kill, and to destroy."

~ St. John 10:10a

In the Book of St. John, Jesus described himself as "the good shepherd" *who giveth life to the sheep"*. He stated in St. John 10:9 *"I am the door: by me if any man enter in, he shall be saved, and shall go in and out, and find pasture"*.

But on the heels of that caring statement about himself, Jesus cautioned in St. John 10:10a that *"the thief cometh not, but for to steal, kill and to destroy"*. In using the word *"thief"*, Jesus is referring to satan.

If you look at the phrase Jesus used at face value only, it can easily make you wonder why he referred to satan as a "thief". The typical view of a thief is someone who opportunistically takes something of value that doesn't belong to them. The World Book Dictionary defines a thief as "one who steals secretly and without force".

Our movie and television industries have given numerous portrayals of thieves, such as the one popularized by the movie series and television shows about "The Pink Panther". If you're in my age category, you probably remember the Pink Panther movies that focused on a character played by actor Peter Sellers in the 1960's and 70's. Seller's character, Inspector Jacques Clouseau, was a bumbling detective in charge of an investigation to find the thief who stole the Pink Panther diamond.

Even though the movie series was about the search for the thief and diamond, the Pink Panther later became associated with the thief, who was played by David Niven in some of the movies. Niven, whose character was called the Phantom, was the coolest thief you could ever imagine. He was smart, cool and calm and went about his business with calculated precision.

For those of you in the younger generation, the well-known actor, comedian and musician, Steve Martin, is the most current actor to play Inspector Clouseau in the Pink Panther movie franchise.

Like in the Pink Panther movies, thieves are typically very intelligent, cool characters who deliberately case out their target before dressing themselves in black to quietly slip into a home or a business during the darkness of night to heist valuables such as jewelry or works of art.

Thieves are generally non-confrontational. They don't want to have to fight their way into getting what they want. They don't want to be involved in a shootout, or have to speed away in a high-powered vehicle to escape the chase of police cars.

Jesus' description of a thief is fitting from the standpoint that the devil is very cunning and subtle when it comes to sneaking in and taking something of value from people.

A perfect example is how he indwelled the serpent and craftily convinced Eve that it was all right for her and Adam to eat from the tree of the knowledge of good and evil. He didn't jump on Eve, pin her down and force a bite of the fruit into her mouth. No. He sweet-talked her. He reasoned with her. He appealed to her natural desire to satisfy the whims of the flesh. And he shrewdly got what he wanted–her separation from God.

"Now the serpent was more subtil than any beast of the field which the Lord God had made. And he said unto the woman, yea, hath God said ye shall not eat of every tree of the garden?

"And the woman said unto the serpent, we may eat of the fruit of the trees of the garden; but of the fruit of the tree which is in the midst of the garden, God hath said, ye shall not eat of it, neither shall ye touch it, lest ye die.

"And the serpent said unto the woman, ye shall not surely die; for God doth know that in the day ye eat thereof, then your eyes shall be opened, and ye shall be as gods, knowing good and evil." (Genesis 3:1-5)

Satan attacks you where you're weak

Satan has always appealed to the human tendency to feed the ego, satisfy self, to live on the edge, to step over the line when it comes to

Chapter 1: The Satanic Conspiracy

authority. And his intellectual reasoning seduced the humanness in Eve to the point of giving in and then influencing Adam to give in, also.

When the Lord questioned Eve about what she had done, she could only admit *"The serpent beguiled me, and I did eat."* (Genesis 3:13)

And not only did she pay a heavy price from the standpoint of herself and Adam being banished from the Garden of Eden, she brought natural and spiritual death upon all of mankind.

Satan's strategy to attack our intellect or mind is something we all must beware of. The Bible warns us that the battleground where our warfare is waged with satan starts in the mind.

"For we wrestle not against flesh and blood, but against principalities (order of powerful angels and demons), against powers, against the rulers of the darkness of this world, against spiritual wickedness in high places (the mind)." (Ephesians 6:12)

This aspect of how the devil attacks people is the reason Jesus called him the father of lies. *"Ye are of your father the devil, and the lusts of your father ye will do; he (the devil) was a murderer from the beginning and abode not in the truth, because there is no truth in him. When he speaketh a lie, he speaketh of his own: for he is a liar, and the father of it."* (John 8:44)

The devil is such a smooth liar; he can talk a mother into trading her baby for money or drugs, a father into forgetting about his family obligations for a sultry woman and a young lady into selling her body for dollar bills.

But Jesus went a step further in describing satan. Not only did he call him a thief who "comes to steal" he also characterized him as someone who comes to "kill and destroy". Stealing is one thing, but killing and destroying; that's a whole other ball game which ups the stakes for all of us.

Shoot em up, bang bang

Robbers are much different than thieves in that they don't mind having to duke it out. They're the ones who don't mind packing weapons, going in and physically or violently taking what they want. Robbers don't mind shooting up the bank or ransacking a home. They don't mind a chase.

Robbers are the macho types. They are chest-pounders who want to get in the face of their victims to demonstrate just how bad they are.

Robbers don't mind killing and destroying to take what they want. They are characterized by such historic figures as Jesse James, Billy the Kid, John Dillinger and Baby Face Nelson. These cold-blooded outlaws would ride into towns with their desperado gangs, intimidate their victims and forcibly take whatever they wanted.

If you're as old as I am, you might remember a popular song by a group called the Intruders. The song was titled *"Cowboys to Girls"*. The first line said:

"I remember when I used to play shoot em up bang-bang. I remember when I'd take the girls and beat em up. But I was young and didn't understand. But now I'm a grown-up man".

When I consider Jesus' description of Satan as a killer and destroyer, it reminds me of those words in that song. It describes how many young people are inclined to take risks or play games with the devil. They generally do it innocently, and naively, not knowing he has a trap waiting to destroy them. All of us adults have been there and that's why it's crucial that we share our learning and knowledge with the young about the devil's real plan.

His real plan is to destroy them any way he can. If he can't do it subtly, he's vicious and bold enough to ride in with his gang of demons to forcibly take what he wants—and that is their futures, here on earth and in Heaven.

That's why the Book of 1 Peter 5:8 warns us *"to be sober, be vigilant because your adversary the devil, as a roaring lion, walketh about seeking whom he may devour."*

Satan is a robber of the most callous kind. He's the king of the jungle, just like the lion who rules the jungle with his power and might.

So why does Jesus warn us about satan being like a thief who comes to steal, kill and destroy? What does the thief He describes want? What is he out to rob from us?

The story in the Book of Daniel about King Nebuchadnezzar, who is a "type" of satan, provides some clear answers about what the "thief" wants.

Keep in mind that much of the Old Testament represents "types and shadows" of things to come. God uses the Old Testament to lay the foundation for what is going to happen in the New Testament and beyond, down to our world and society today and even into the future.

I like to refer to the Old Testament as "God's Word concealed" where much typology or symbolism is used to illustrate how God worked and the New Testament as "God's Word revealed" where he explains exactly what he means.

Consequently, to best understand satan's strategy to steal, kill and destroy the future and eternal destinies of our youth, it's important to recognize the symbolism behind Nebuchadnezzar and Babylon of the Old Testament. Nebuchadnezzar represents satan and Babylon represents the "world" or the worldly system.

Nebuchadnezzar Is After My Child

Chapter 2

To Kidnap And To Conquer

"And the king spake unto Ashpenaz the master of his eunuchs, that he should bring certain of the children of Israel, and of the king's seed, and of the princes."

~ *Daniel 1:3*

Nebuchadnezzar was the wicked king who reigned many, many years ago over the ancient city of Babylon. He's mentioned around 90 times in the Bible, but is featured most prominently in the Book of Daniel.

Nebuchadnezzar ruled from 605 BC (Before Christ) until approximately 562 BC and is considered the greatest king of the Babylonian Empire. In Biblical history, Nebuchadnezzar is most famous for conquering Judah and the ultimate destruction of Judah and Jerusalem in 586 BC.

It was Nebuchadnezzar's first year (605 BC) as king when he initially conquered Judah and made it pay tribute (submissive fees) to him. At that time, he took hostage royal personnel, including Daniel, Hananiah, Azariah and Mishael, and temple treasures back to Babylon (Daniel 1:1-7). This began Judah's 70-year captivity, which had been predicted by the prophet Jeremiah (Jeremiah 25:11-12).

In 597 BC during the reign of Jehoiachin, Judah rebelled against the Babylonian rule. Nebuchadnezzar responded by invading Jerusalem again, resulting in King Jehoiachin, the rest of the temple treasures, and 10,000 more men, including the prophet Ezekiel, being carried away to Babylon.

However, in 586 BC, during the reign of King Zedekiah, Judah again rebelled. When that happened, Nebuchadnezzar got fed up with the rebellions, and believed Judah had not learned its lesson when he first invaded, conquered, and deported many of them in 597 BC.

Consequently, he and his general, Nebuzaradan, invaded Jerusalem, the capital of Judah, for the final time; this time completely destroying the temple, the bulk of the city and deporting King Zedekiah and most of the remaining residents to Babylon.

In this, according to Jeremiah 25:9, Nebuchadnezzar served as God's instrument of judgment on Judah for its idolatry, unfaithfulness, and disobedience.

Historically, Babylon was called the Neo-Babylonian Empire (II Kings 24:1). It broke the supremacy of Assyria and dominated the world from 605 BC to 539 BC. The Babylonian Empire lasted about 70 years, the same 70 years the nation of Judah was in captivity. Nebuchadnezzar was the tyrannical ruler during Babylon's reign over Judah.

Babylon was the mightiest metropolis the ancient world had ever known. It was largely built by the efforts of Hammurabi and Nebuchadnezzar II. It declined with the fall of Nebuchadnezzar, fell to a lower level under Belshazzar, and came to ruin about 130 BC at the hand of the Parthians.

In modern day vernacular, during its heyday, Babylon was the "hottest" city in the land. It was New York and Los Angeles rolled into one. It was where people went to party, to seek out knowledge and to become known. It was the place where the rich and famous hung out, the place where dreams and ambitions were played out – sometimes no matter what the costs. If you lived in Babylon, you were considered somebody and you thought you were on top of the world.

This explains why many Biblical scholars believe the Tower of Babel was constructed somewhere in the territory of Babylon, where Nimrod, the grandson of Noah developed his kingdom. The name Nimrod implies one who is a rebel and it's believed it was during his time that people began to rebel against God. Small wonder, they decided to build the Tower of Babel.

Look at what they said. *". . . go to, let us build us a city and a tower, whose top may reach unto heaven; and let us make us a name, lest we be scattered abroad upon the face of the whole earth."* (Genesis 11:4)

The desire of these people was to dominate the world and determine their own destiny apart from God through man-centered organizational unity, power and great accomplishments. This purpose was based on pride

Chapter 2: To Kidnap And To Conquer

and rebellion against God (Full Study Bible: page 23). The result was that God destroyed their foolish effort and multiplied their language so that some could no longer communicate with each other.

Simply put, Babylon's monarchs believed they should be the ones to rule the world. That's why King Nebuchadnezzar conquered Judah. He wanted to rule the world, and that started with subjugating the nation which claimed to be God's chosen people. And the King knew that an effective strategy to take control would be to bring the Hebrew youth into captivity and change them from servants of God into what he wanted them to be.

The key word here is **"change"**. The whole purpose of satan is to change a person from following after God, His precepts and principles, into a carnal, fleshly-minded sinner, bent on satisfying only himself or herself.

This is in direct contradiction with what God wants to accomplish in our lives. God's purpose is to "change" us from a sinner to a Saint, back into the image of Himself.

"Therefore, if any man be in Christ, he is a new creature: old things are passed away; behold, all things are become new." (II Corinthians 5:17)

Taking over the land

In his attempt to change the Hebrew hostages, King Nebuchadnezzar needed to take away their culture. That started with him besieging, or taking over their city, and then controlling everything in it. That's typical of how the devil wanted to take over the throne of God and now wants to control God's people on planet earth.

This is significant related to the premise of this book because it is consistent with the spirit that exists within the world today. It's a spirit that stems from the heart of satan himself and one that he has and is desperately attempting to infuse within the hearts and minds of youth all over the world.

I contend this is the controlling spirit that has infiltrated the minds of many of our youth today. Too many young people, barely big enough to see over the dashboard of a vehicle, want to be in control of everything around them, the home, their schools, and their communities.

How many conversations have you had with people or have heard while sitting around in a doctor's office, hair salon or restaurant about how your child or someone else's child has tried to take over the house. They want to watch what they want to watch on television. They want to eat what they want to eat at dinner and between meals. They want to come and go as they please. They want to get up when they please and go to bed when they please. They don't want to follow any rules set by their parents.

And then when the parent challenges their child about their behavior, the response today of many children is one of defiance, a scowl, a stomping away or an outright verbal assault against the parent's authority to even ask them to do something they don't want to do.

Parents don't want the conflict

I maintain that far too many parents have caved in or given in to this struggle for power and control. They've gotten tired of constant conflict, the continual "fighting with their kids" and have decided largely as a result of popular, modern psychological teaching that it's "better" to be friends with their kids; that it's better to give their children the responsibility to make decisions for themselves.

That sounds very good on the surface. But further examination shows that it really hasn't worked. What has happened in many instances is that the children end up living on one end of the house, doing whatever they well please and the parents living on the other end of the house hoping that the kids don't kill themselves before they come to their senses.

The sad and sobering consequences of this form of "independent" living were vividly illustrated in a 1999 Public Broadcast Service television documentary entitled *"The Lost Children of Rockdale County"*.

The documentary cast the spotlight on a syphilis epidemic in the quiet, upper-middle class Atlanta, Ga., suburb of Conyers. The documentary chronicled the lives of a group of Conyers' teenagers as they frolicked about from bed to bed, freely engaging in sexual activities with each other like it was giving each other hugs or handshakes.

The documentary featured interviews with teens who claimed to have had as many as 100 sexual partners—or joined in group sex parties. Some of those teens reported becoming sexually active as early as 12 years old.

Chapter 2: To Kidnap And To Conquer

One of the girls involved in the sex ring said in an article about the documentary "I mean, sex is just a thing. It's no big deal anymore. It's just a thing. It's just like going to school every day, getting up and going to school. Oh, you know, you meet this guy, 'Let's have sex'. That's just how it is with people now".

The sad result of their promiscuity was the outbreak of the syphilis epidemic that infected 17 teenagers in Rockdale County—some as young as 13—and forced 250 others to get medical treatment.

Even sadder was that the parents of the teenagers and the entire county learned about the outbreak on national television. According to a CNN Health web report, when the news hit the local newspaper, parents and the community were "horrified".

"My question is—where are the parents who set limits as to what are . . . acceptable behaviors and what is not?" Bill Hughey, who is now retired but at the time was with the Rockdale Coalition for Children and Families, stated in the CNN Health report.

One mother quoted in the PBS documentary poignantly stated: "I think what it is, is we've lost control of our children".

The tragedy was that in a sparkling, upper-class, suburban city, the parents of the children let them have far too much freedom to do as they pleased.

The problem with giving teenagers free reign to do as they please is that they generally don't have the level of maturity yet to make the best decisions. Some young people do mature faster than others do, but it is the rare one whom is able to make adult type decisions before they are fully adults.

Consequently, the documentary about the syphilis outbreak in Conyers points up a more far-reaching problem. Way too many of our children are negatively impacting their lives in one way or the other long before they've reached a stable level of maturity. The startling statistics on teenage suicides, drug use, abuse and overdoses, alcohol use and abuse and teenage pregnancy all paint the grim picture that children are not mature enough to have control.

Chapter 3

The Fight For Control

"Children, obey your parents in the Lord: for this is right."

~ Ephesians 6:1

I remember the time my three children attempted to effect a coup d'etat (takeover) in our home. They had every intention of dethroning me as the head of the home. I still wonder if they hadn't plotted their insurrection for several years before they tried to carry it out.

Thank God that his spirit within me revealed their plan to me in time that I was able to maintain control. I can still see the fear on their faces as I backed them into the hallway wall. I'm sure they thought I'd gone mad and was on the verge of taking them out as I appropriately raised my voice for emphasis to let them know that I was not going to let them take over the home.

I emphatically explained to them that the devil himself was behind their attempted uprising and that I by no means was going to relinquish the authority of the home that God had obligated me to. They were not going to play "their music" as loud as they wanted. They were not going to clean up after themselves when they felt like it. They were not going to do as they pleased.

I told them that even though they didn't like the rules of the house, they were there because of the love I and their mother had for them and they were set for their own good. I said that I wasn't going to allow the devil to come in and ride roughshod over them and that I was going to do everything within my power to protect them as best I could.

The coup attempt by my children came when they were around the ages of 10, 12 and 14. But it can happen with children at varying ages. It's a sad thing to see when you visit someone's house and it's clear that the children are in control.

Children use a variety of tactics in their attempts to seize control of the household. Some are intimidation, fear and even physical violence. Because of this, there are many parents who live in a state of anxiety in their own homes. They're afraid to leave the home for fear of what would go on when they're away. And they're afraid to stay home because of the intimidation that the child is using against them. And perhaps worse of all is many are afraid to go to sleep at night, for fear of the child committing bodily harm to them.

One case I've been personally involved in is one of the worst I've heard or read about. There were four children in the family, two boys and two girls. The oldest son had joined the military and was out of the house. It was after he left that the younger teenage son rose up to seize control.

At first, he tried to form an alliance with the oldest daughter. But the parents were able to quell her rebellion before it became too overbearing. The son, however, was unrelenting. He was totally out of control. He cursed his parents. He physically abused them. And he stole so much from them; they were forced to put deadbolt locks on their bedroom doors. But these didn't stop him from getting in through windows.

The boy joined a street gang and dealt drugs. He didn't make it through a full year of school without getting kicked out from the time he started middle school. The police had to be called time and time again to the home to stop a violent episode.

The most appalling part of all this is the time the father was handcuffed and carted off to jail because he'd put several bruises and scratches on the boy while subduing him during a violent, physical outbreak.

Now doesn't that take the cake? A father who subdues his own son because of a violent outbreak in the home ends up being the one to go to jail. It shows how far our society—even through our laws—has given in to this spirit of children taking control.

I believe America is unquestionably the best place to live in the world based on the vast opportunities that exist here. But I also believe it has gone way overboard when it comes to the so-called, constitutional freedoms it insists its people are entitled to. These constitutional freedoms have resulted in prayer being taken out of school, disciplinary authority

Chapter 3: The Fight For Control

being taken out of the hands of teachers and even to a large extent out of the hands of parents.

I'll always remember the story a past coworker of mine related to me. She said she'd read an article which reported the sad story of what a high school principle said before a school athletic event. The principal informed those in the stands that from a legal and constitutional position, her school could:

- distribute condoms to students; and
- provide students rides to abortion clinics where they could receive abortions without their parents' knowledge or consent.

But, the principal said in spite of all the things her school could do, she lamented that she could not allow the students to be led in prayer, which is in direct conflict with the God-fearing, religious creed of "in God we trust" our great country was founded upon.

A teacher who cared

One of the most distressing examples I've seen of the frustration of today's teachers was after I released the book *"Looking For A Place In The Sun"*. For those of you who read it, you'll recall that I talked about how one of the turning points in my life was brought on by my ninth grade English teacher. I call her Mrs. Willis in the book, but her real name is Mrs. Brown.

Mrs. Brown was the first person who ever told me I had the potential to make something good out of my life. It was the comments Mrs. Brown wrote on a report I had submitted which became the first motivating force for me to pursue going beyond the auto factories and steel mills that the people I knew were destined to spend the bulk of their lives in.

It was her words which initially triggered in me a drive to excel, to pursue bigger things in life. At the time, I had no idea where I could go or how I could get there, but a fire was lit inside me and it's still burning today.

After publishing the book, I was determined to find Mrs. Brown and thank her for caring enough about me to push me, to encourage me and light a fire within my soul. I hadn't seen Mrs. Brown since I left her ninth grade class, a span of 25 years. But I found her, still teaching, still trying her best to motivate students, still trying to inspire them to reach for the stars.

She was teaching at the high school where I graduated. She graciously left her desk and talked with me at the door. I noticed that she was hesitant to completely leave the room so we kind of chatted while standing in the doorway between the classroom and hallway. I understood her reluctance to leave the room after our talk, which left both of us teary-eyed.

"I'm so glad you came back to tell me I was able to inspire you," she told me. "I just wish it were like it used to be. It's really hard to motivate students today. All the majority of them seem to want to do is come to class and take a nap. They're so much different from students back when you were in school. They're undisciplined and demotivated. It can be very discouraging."

As Mrs. Brown spoke with me, my eyes scanned the room behind her. Most of the students were either slouched in their seats or had their heads lying on the top of the desks. Their eyes reflected their disinterest. There were no gleams, no twinkles, just a dull redness that told me they couldn't see beyond the bleakness of the day they were living in.

Unfortunately, that wasn't the last time I would see that sad scene at Mrs. Brown's classroom. I've seen it at many other schools I've been fortunate enough to visit and talk with students about pursuing their place in the sun.

The lack of ambition, and perhaps more importantly the lack of discipline, among many young people in our schools and homes has become a major drawback to their success in life. It's something many of them don't learn during their early years and are unable to practice when they get older.

I believe one reason they don't learn it is the prevailing attitude about how it should be taught, particularly as it relates to "corporal" punishment.

Our modern-day, free thinking society has decided that it's no longer good for teachers to "paddle" undisciplined and unruly students. Many opponents to paddling advocate that it protects a child's physical and emotional health. Consequently, paddling is now widely considered "abuse" and has been banned in at least 31 states in America.

Chapter 3: The Fight For Control

Worse than that is the fact that our government has literally stolen the authority parents were given by God when it comes to how they are able to discipline their children in their own homes.

There have been several cases where parents have been arrested for physically disciplining their children. You may have heard of the story about Adrian Peterson, a star running back in the National Football League, who reached a plea agreement to a charge of child abuse involving his four-year-old son. Peterson was charged as a result of disciplining his son with a switch, something that was common in the Texas culture he grew up in.

It also should be noted that paddling children was still legal in the state of Texas at that time.

According to police reports, Peterson's son suffered multiple injuries, such as welts, from the whipping, and Peterson acknowledged the injuries. However, he stressed he had no intent of abusing his son, but only to teach him discipline in the same manner he was taught it by his parents.

Peterson was quoted in an exclusive CBS Houston television report on September 12, 2014 that "he loves all his kids, and only "whups" them because he wants them to do right. Toward the end of the interview, Peterson said he would reconsider using switches in the future, but said he would never "eliminate whupping my kids. . . because I know how being spanked has helped me in my life."

Peterson further told CBS Houston that "deep in my heart I have always believed I could have been one of those kids that was lost in the streets without the discipline instilled in me by my parents and other relatives. I have always believed that the way my parents disciplined me has a great deal to do with the success I have enjoyed as a man. I love my son and I will continue to become a better parent and learn from any mistakes I ever make."

Unfortunately, our modern society doesn't agree with the Biblical and what used to be the traditional way of disciplining children and Peterson paid a hefty price. Even though he was able to reach a plea deal that downgraded a felony charge to a misdemeanor that carried a $4,000 fine and an order to perform community service, he was suspended a year without pay by the NFL, resulting in the loss of millions of dollars.

More recently, a June 2016 USA Today article reported that a New Orleans, La. mother was arrested for whipping her three sons—after she caught them burglarizing a home.

The mother was quoted in the article that "I never could imagine trying to be a good mother would end me up in jail with a criminal record like I'm a predator out to hurt my kids, who I live for. That's my world. Everything revolves around them. Everything I do is for my kids."

It may not have cost this mother millions of dollars like it did Adrian Peterson, but the message her arrest carries is the same: the devil is waging an all-out attack to eliminate the principles of parenting set by God in terms of disciplining children.

And, it's giving children the upper hand when it comes to control, so much so that children have gotten to the point where they don't hesitate to call the 911 line to report that their parents have whipped them or are about to whip them.

And when the call is made, the police come running. Parents are arrested and sometimes jailed. Their reputations are tarnished and their kids end up with authority over the home, free to do whatever they want to do.

All this in spite of the fact that the Bible says *"Withhold not correction from the child; for if thou beatest him with the rod, he shall not die. Thou shalt beat him with the rod, and shalt deliver his soul from hell."* (Proverbs 23:13&14)

In fact, according to the Bible, if you don't whip your child, it's akin to hating him or her. Look at this. *"He that spareth his rod hateth his son; but he that loveth him chasteneth him betimes."* (Proverbs 13:24)

Now, I'm certainly not advocating child abuse. Nor, is the Bible advocating abusing your children. It isn't saying that a parent should take out their anger on a child. It's talking about applying physical discipline in a reasonable manner that makes a good enough impression on the child that he or she recognizes right from wrong and that there are consequences to their actions.

I would be the first to defend the Biblical principle of *"sparing not the rod"*. But I would also be the first to say parents should not use the rod to the extent that it becomes abusive. Children can tell when a parent

Chapter 3: The Fight For Control

"whips" them for disciplinary reasons and it's done out of love. They also can tell when a parent is "whipping" them or "hitting" them out of anger or contempt.

I'm sure many parents have learned, just like I did, that if your child feels they can do wrong, or "act up" like we're fond of saying, they will do their wrongful deeds over and over again.

I fully understand the popular, psychological concept of "time out" that was popularized in the 1970's as an alternative to spanking. Time-out, which is also known as "social exclusion" is a form of behavioral modification that involves temporarily separating a child from an environment where unwanted behavior according to the cultural standards and values of the time and place has occurred with the goal of stopping the offending behavior *(from parents.com article).*

The Time-Out concept was just one of the many new-age child psychology concepts that emerged in the latter part of the 20th century that helped diminish the Biblical instruction related to spanking children. But with the assortment of issues negatively impacting our youth exacerbating, even that concept is now being questioned. A more recent parents.com article noted that some opponents of the concept have recommended banning it altogether (source: parents.com article).

Generally, in my view, all the time-out process did for little Johnny or Sue was give them a chance to catch their breath for the next round of terror.

The questionable laws our country has placed on the books regarding child-abuse have tied the hands of well-meaning, God-fearing parents and teachers in America. These child abuse laws are designed to hold individuals who harm children legally accountable for their actions. These laws are directed at parents, guardians, caretakers, and anyone else responsible for a child's well-being. Child abuse is not limited to physical harm.

Most child abuse statutes also include emotional harm, sexual abuse or exploitation, as well as acts or failures to act that result in an imminent risk of danger to the child. Allegations of child abuse can result in criminal charges and/or the initiation of a child neglect case in civil court. Statutes prohibiting child abuse have been enacted at the state and federal level.

People are arrested on charges of child abuse every day in the United States. Many of these individuals did in fact cause harm to a child and deserve to be dealt with accordingly. However, others end up on the wrong side of the law by mistake.

Teachers and other professionals have a legal responsibility to report incidents that tend to suggest any kind of abuse, and law enforcement officers do not hesitate to take action when there is a possibility of preventing harm to a child. This willingness to error on the side of protecting kids is laudable. Unfortunately, though, it results in a number of child abuse cases that are simply without merit (source: HG.org).

The issue here is that Christian parents, or any parents for that matter, who love their children desperately want to do the right things when it comes to raising them according to the tenets of God. But they are often afraid of fully following through for fear of losing the friendship many psychologists say they should have with their children; or even worse of being arrested and taken to court for being accused of physically abusing them.

It's a catch-22 situation that the devil has put parents in. And he's standing back laughing at the mental and emotional struggle Christian parents are going through when it comes to child rearing and relishing the fact that he's effectively stolen control.

Satan has always wanted control

A child's desire to have control stems directly from the heart of the devil. It is what caused him to form that wicked alliance with a third of the angels in Heaven and attempt to overthrow God.

Although Satan's attempt to seize control of Heaven failed, he brought that same ambition down to planet earth. If he couldn't take control from God, then he'd take control of the man that God made, and infuse in that man the same wicked desire to have control.

There are several Biblical examples of offspring that were influenced by satan's prodding to seize control. One of the more prominent ones is the son of King David named Absalom. The story of Absalom's attempt to seize control of Israel is found in the book of II Samuel. Look at chapter 15, verses four through six.

"Absalom said moreover, Oh that I were made judge in the land, that every man which hath any suit or cause might come unto me, and I would do him justice!

"And it was so, that when any man came nigh to him to do him obeisance, he put forth his hand and took him, and kissed him.

"And on this manner did Absalom to all Israel that came to the king for judgement: so Absalom stole the hearts of the men of Israel."

The problem, however, with young people rising up against their parents is they are blinded to the vengeance that God will exact on them. God will always avenge his people, especially those parents who strive to teach their children the laws of God and raise them accordingly.

Absalom was no exception. Even though he succeeded for a time in winning the hearts of the people of Israel, it was short-lived. It wasn't long before his life was taken and the peoples' hearts turned back to David (II Samuel 16).

When a seed for control is sown in a person's heart, one consequence is that it blinds the person. It is so pervasive; it prevents them from seeing clearly. In Lucifer's case, the blinding ambition to control heaven was so strong, it blinded him from the absolute reality that it was impossible for him to defeat the omnipotent God who was the creator of all things.

Nebuchadnezzar Is After My Child

Chapter 4

What Kind Of Attitude Is This?

Adolescence is a period of rapid changes. Between the ages of 12 and 17, for example, a parent ages as much as 20 years.

~ Author Unknown

The controlling spirit obsessing many of our young people has pervaded every area of our society. It can be seen in the casual style of dress that prevails among young people, who feel they can dress in such casual style even to conduct job interviews. It often can be seen it their indifferent treatment of customers at fast food restaurants and lack of respect for older adults and authority figures.

In a January 31, 2000 USA Today article, Family Therapist and Author Carleton Kendrick called this behavior by teens "attitude". "Attitude" is characterized by modern-day teen buzz words such as "Whatever," "Well, hell-O, "What's it to you?" It's also shown in "the look," a scowl that can be more condemning than words. There's the defiantly silent body language; the I'd rather be-any-where-but-here-attitude.

The USA Today article said parenting experts believe it's the parent's role to define acceptable behavior, but teen lip would be easier for parents to handle if they understood where it was coming from. It added, "teen lip, attitude or surliness can be very painful—and inexplicable—to parents".

The child psychologists, family therapists and other experts quoted in the USA Today article said the surliness of teens—my wife calls it saltiness—stems from their living in a "pressure cooker". The experts said teens constantly feel as if there's a spotlight on them, and that peers, teachers, coaches and parents are evaluating them.

The experts say parents often misinterpret surliness as aloofness when actually it's vulnerability. Kendrick said, "it's just the way teenagers react to all the turmoil that's going on inside them".

The experts quoted in the USA Today article said parents use a variety of parenting styles to cope with surly teens:

- The **angry parent** who gets angry and tries to control their child with that anger. The angry parent lashes out at their child by using such phrases as "you are nothing but a little ingrate for treating me like this".
- The **helicopter parent**, who "hovers" around the child all the time. This type of parent swoops in before the mouthiness ever starts. However, the experts say "when parents rescue teens from their own bad behavior, the kids never experience things, learn from the consequences and act better the next time."
- The **emotionally absent parent**, who has gotten tired of parenting by the time their child is a teenager. Their career may be very demanding, so when the child begins pushing them away, the parents abdicate some of their responsibility.
- The **respectful, understanding parent**, who is able to set limits while still treating their children with respect and empathy. These are the parents who when they see a look of aloofness, nastiness or a detached attitude on their child's face, they step back and don't take it personally.

New millennium parenting style

A February 12, 2001 Time magazine article reported on a new millennium style of parental discipline. It's called the new "Time Out". This theory, promoted by Boston psychologist Anthony Wolf in his book *The Secret of Parenting*, says when it comes to disciplining children, parents should exercise the "time out" principle earlier psychologists said parents should use on their children.

Wolf says parents often fall into a trap in which when their children misbehave badly, they resort to punishing them out of anger, frustration or the lack of an alternative idea.

"A parent should not rise to the bait," Wolf says. "My wife and I had this thing we did with our kids when they were trying to provoke us. We'd just look at them calmly and say 'Goodbye,' and then go about our business."

I have to agree with Wolf's line of thinking when it comes to the fact that parents often get angry with their children when they misbehave and often don't know what to do in terms of discipline.

Chapter 4: What Kind of Attitude Is This?

I went through that myself. It reminds me of the time my boys did something that was totally unacceptable. To this day, I don't remember what it was that they did. What I do recall is the difficulty I had in deciding what would be the most appropriate discipline to mete out.

I don't remember a time I was more upset with those guys who were only six and eight at the time. I knew I had to do something to get through to them the severity of what they'd done. And I also knew, it couldn't be killing them, if they were to remember it.

In the midst of my shaking from the anger that had welled inside, an out of the box thought I believe was prompted by the Spirit of God jumped into my mind. Take the boys fishing. Get yourself calmed down and talk to them.

So that's what I did. I took them out to one of the local reservoirs. It was calming sitting on the bank of the reservoir on the warm Ohio early evening, even though we only got an occasional bite.

I sat there a long time, just listening to the soothing sounds of the water lapping against the banks of the shore; the wind rustling the leaves of trees; the birds chirping and cawing as they chased insects; and the crickets playing their mating songs by clicking their heels together.

It was times like this while sitting on the bank of a river or reservoir when I most understood why many of the Bible stories centered around water and its soothing effects on the souls of men.

After a couple of hours of sitting and talking, mostly mine about the severity of what they had done, another thought—prompted by the Spirit —came to me. Take the boys to the church and pray for them.

So that's what I did. We packed up our rods, reels and leftover bait and I took them to the church I attended at the time. I had a key since I was one of the ministers.

Once inside, I gathered the boys up at the altar and reiterated to them how bad what they had done was and how that kind of behavior could not be tolerated. I told them how disappointed I was in their actions and what I initially wanted to do to them, but couldn't because I knew it was wrong.

I told them that in situations like this, all I could do was rely on God to show me how to correct them and He had said to bring them to Him and pray that He intervene. So that's what I did. I prayed for those boys, that they would recognize their misbehavior and try their best to be better.

I prayed that God would open up their minds, even at such a tender age, to live the kind of lifestyle He wanted all of us to live and that was in obedience to His Word.

After the prayer, I let them know I loved them, but also that I expected them to do their best to be what God wanted them to be.

This was just one of the methods I used in my attempts to properly raise my children, teach them discipline and instill in them God's laws. I believe I tried every parental trick in the book and many that weren't in the book. And, as I noted, I did so as the Spirit of God led me.

But I also believed that the rod was definitely an appropriate and allowable tool that God has given parents to use to discipline our children, and as my children will tell you, I used it on more than one occasion.

What the Bible says we have to be careful about is provoking our children to wrath. Ephesians 6:4 states *"And ye fathers, provoke not your children to wrath: but bring them up in the nurture and admonition of the Lord"*.

Provoke means to "excite to anger or resentment" or "to stir to action of feeling". Wrath means "furious, often vindictive anger; rage".

So what God warns parents about is not to excite or stir up feelings or actions in their children that could lead them to become furious or filled with vindictive anger.

I believe parents can provoke their children to wrath in a variety of ways. I won't go into the broad spectrum of them. I'll just give several examples, including one of the times I felt provoked to wrath when I was young.

My parents didn't attend my little league baseball games or junior high sporting events. When I'd see my teammates' parents rooting for them it caused resentment to germinate and grow inside me against my parents.

That's why when I was the star running back of the football team during senior year in high school I resented my father for making sure everybody in the stands knew "that's my son". After all, he hadn't come to any of my games when I was much younger and needed a father figure supporting and encouraging me like my teammates did.

Chapter 4: What Kind of Attitude Is This?

Sure, I understand now that my father was very busy working two and three jobs to support his large family and just didn't have many opportunities to attend my games. But I didn't recognize that at the time. It just excited me to vindictive anger.

Parents can often unknowingly provoke their children to wrath by ignoring their pleas for attention, their requests for time, their overtures for love.

Inside all children is an innate desire for attention from their parents. And when they don't get it, it's easy for them to resent their parents and search for the attention they crave from other people. This could be positive or it could be negative, depending on the influences the child gives in to.

One of the reasons many children gravitate to gangs or unscrupulous groups is they're craving for attention or to have a sense of belonging.

Another way parents can provoke their children to wrath is through verbal abuse. Have you ever heard a parent say to a child "I'm going to kill you" or "you're never going to amount to anything" or "you're nothing but a little animal" or "you're ugly".

I believe making comments like these can have an equally or even more damaging effect on a child as not giving them the attention they need.

Parents have to realize that the things they verbally sow or plant into their children's heads when they are young can have a direct impact on the person they ultimately become. That's why the Bible says *"Thou art snared with the words of thy mouth, thou art taken with the words of thy mouth"* (Proverbs 6:2).

Parents can also provoke their children to wrath through physical abuse. We have to be very careful when it comes to how we deal with our children through physical means.

I discussed earlier the Biblical principle related to spanking children and making sure it doesn't reach the level of abuse. Here, I want to address the issue of parents physically fighting their children.

My philosophy as a parent was never to put myself in a position where I would have to literally "fight" one of my children. When they got to the point where they were too old or too large to "whip" I had to discipline them in other ways, such as taking away privileges.

I understood very well that when boys start feeling their oats the temptation they have—just like many of us men had at one time or another—that they can "take" their father. Both my boys grew to be larger than I am. And, during their high school years, they were football players who lifted weights nearly year-round. I knew they were stronger than I was. I also knew if I ever got into a "fight" with one of them, something regretful would likely happen because I knew I was not going to let them whip me.

Were there ever times fights almost occurred between one of my sons and me? Yes. Did I ever have to grab one of them by the collar, lift them off the floor and put their back up against a wall to let him know who was in charge? Yes. There were times when things got extremely heated between one of my sons and me.

But did I ever hit them like I was fighting another man? A resounding no! Every time, in the back of my mind, I was praying and believing God that He would intervene and provide a way of escape from the heated situation. And He always did.

So the approach I took was never to promote fighting in the household. I never let my boys "play fight" or wrestle with each other. I'd seen and heard about too many occasions when play fighting turned into real fights between brothers or cousins or friends. I've also heard, and you may have to, about fathers killing their sons or brothers killing their brothers after one has been provoked by the other.

I didn't believe in wrestling with them either after they got over 10 years old. I felt it was important that I do whatever I could to keep the thought out of my sons' heads that they should ever fight with their siblings or with me. That just was not the proper thing to do.

Whatever the case may be—emotional, verbal or physical abuse—parents have to be very careful to avoid provoking their children to wrath. It can create scars on a child for life.

Think about the type of person you are. I'm sure you can point to things your parents said about you or did to you that had an influence on who you are today. The worst thing about it is that there are many adults who

Chapter 4: What Kind of Attitude Is This?

are living out their lives in mental hospitals or wandering the streets of cities as a result of being mentally deranged by the things they heard as children or by the things that were done to them.

As parents, it is vital that we plant good, positive, wholesome thoughts into our children's heads from the time they are born. It's our job to instill in them the fact that they are treasures, created by God for His glory and purpose.

I previously listed the parenting styles experts say parents use to deal with surly teenagers. However, psychologist generally agree there are four standard, major recognized parenting styles: authoritative, neglectful, permissive, and authoritarian.

Authoritative parenting is widely regarded as the most effective and beneficial parenting style for normal children. Authoritative parents are easy to recognize, as they are marked by the high expectations that they have of their children, but temper these expectations with understanding and support for their children as well.

Neglectful parenting is one of the most harmful styles of parenting that can be used on a child. Neglectful parenting is unlike the other styles in that parents have little emotional involvement with their kids. While providing for their basic needs, they are uninvolved in their children's lives.

Permissive parenting, also known as indulgent parenting is another potentially harmful style of parenting. These parents are responsive but not demanding. These parents tend to be lenient while trying to avoid confrontation. The benefit of this parenting style is that they are usually very nurturing and loving. The negatives, however, outweigh this benefit. Few rules are set for the children of permissive parents, and the rules are inconsistent when they do exist. This lack of structure causes these children to grow up with little self-discipline and self-control.

Authoritarian parenting, also called strict parenting, is characterized by parents who are demanding but not responsive. Authoritarian parents allow for little open dialogue between parent and child and expect children to follow a strict set of rules and expectations. They usually rely on punishment to demand obedience or teach a lesson (my.vanderbilt.edu).

Have you noticed the type of parenting style you use? I've talked with parents who fit into each of the categories listed. I believe the ideal approach a parent can take is what works best for them, based on sound Biblical principles. I personally used a combination of many approaches, all based on the circumstances at the time, as well as based on the personality of the child.

I'm not a psychologist, but as a licensed minister I've counseled with many parents over the past thirty years. And I completely agree with the experts' opinion that our teenagers have a war waging on the inside.

Our society is changing almost as fast as the speed of sound. Technology has taken them into the future today. They're exposed to things by the time they're five that many of us weren't exposed to until our teenage years or beyond.

They've seen televised images of students gunned down unmercifully at schools around the country. They've seen wars in which thousands of military personnel and civilians have died. They've seen their parents lose jobs. They've seen their parents split up. They've seen immorality occur at the highest levels of government.

So yes, teenagers and young adults do have a lot to deal with. There is more pressure on them than ever. But I contend it's turmoil that goes far deeper than the "pressure" teens feel from their social surroundings.

The Biblical reality of it is, the inner turmoil that our teens and young adults feel is primarily due to an absent relationship with God and an all out attack by satan to steal their future and their souls.

Chapter 5

Satan Wants To Get 'Em In Their Prime

"And the king spake unto Ashpenaz the master of his eunuchs, that he should bring certain of the children of Israel, and of the king's seed, and of the princes.."

~ Daniel 1:3

It's extremely important for Christian parents to recognize that no matter how good they are as parents, the devil is still going to attack their children in some way, shape or form.

In today's society, satan is using a variety of methods, some blatant, some subtle to attach his tentacles around the lives of our youth. The strategy that King Nebuchadnezzar used in Bible days is a model for how satan is operating in our world today.

Nebuchadnezzar used a diabolical step-by-step process in his attempt to destroy the youth in his day. The first criteria he set was for his henchmen to take away the best and brightest young men of Israel from their cherished homeland (Daniel, chapter 1, verses 3-4)).

"And the king spake unto Ashpenaz the master of his eunuchs, that he should bring certain of the children of Israel, and of the king's seed, and of the princes;

"Children in whom was no blemish, but well favored, and skillful in all wisdom, and cunning in knowledge, and understanding science, and such as had ability in them to stand in the king's palace, and whom they might teach the learning and the tongue of the Chaldeans."

By today's standards, these "certain" young men are our sons and daughters whom we've raised up in the church. They are that first, second and third generation of young people whose parents nursed them on church pews, had them in noon-day and Friday night prayer meetings,

Wednesday Bible studies and Monday evening street meetings or outreach services.

They are the generation of young people who grew up largely shielded from the environment of the world; those who generally weren't allowed to run the streets or permitted to attend what were generally considered "worldly functions" like middle or high school dances.

But the problem stems from the fact that while we parents are doing all we know to protect our children from the beggarly elements of the world; we often fail to realize how difficult it is for them as they stand between two worlds. On the one hand, they are torn by the powerful influences they are surrounded by when they're away from the Christian confines of home or church. On the other hand, they're trying in their own youthful way to stay true to their upbringing.

I discovered this reality when my children first started attending school. It was very unsettling when they began coming home different, talking different and thinking different. At first, I didn't understand what was happening. Then the Lord opened my eyes.

My children were suddenly being exposed to a world that was different from what they knew at home. The Christian environment in the home and church formerly had been all they were familiar with.

Now, they were interacting with many children who didn't come from the same incubated Christian environment. These kids talked differently. They acted differently. They were different.

And now my children were faced with a dilemma of which they didn't fully know how to respond. Like most young people, they wanted to be accepted. They wanted to fit in, and the only way they knew how was to start taking on the nature of the other kids they now were surrounded by.

They started acting like or similar to the children they were around, and the worst part of it all was that they started bringing that behavior and mindset into the home.

It is very important for Christian parents to understand the plight our children are put in when they start attending non-Christian public or private schools. They're suddenly thrust into a world where many of the values and morals they'd been diligently taught as preschoolers now aren't so prominent.

Chapter 5: Satan Wants To Get 'Em In Their Prime

They are around many children who don't have the same upbringing as they do; children who don't include God or Jesus in their conversations, let alone in their lives. They are sitting next to and playing with children who are accustomed to hearing profanity in and around the house, who are accustomed to alcoholic beverages being consumed in the home, accustomed to explicit secular music and television shows being regularly listened to and watched.

They find themselves in a different world they feel uncomfortable and out of place in. And now they have a mental and emotional fight on their hands, a fight their youthful state of maturity is not completely prepared to wage.

The end result is they occasionally make naïve mistakes, like children are prone to do. In the particular case of my oldest son, some of these naïve mistakes cost him significant time in suspension from public school and off the football team he loved. It also cost a substantial amount of his parent's income to pay for him to attend private school.

Pew babies are primary targets

While satan's overriding goal is to destroy all youth, his primary targets are those who have been raised in the church, those who have a Christian foundation. He is particularly interested in attacking these young people because he recognizes their vast potential to be the church leaders of the future.

The book of Daniel gives a vivid description, through the operation of Nebuchadnezzar, exactly how the devil targets pew babies from day one. He wants to destroy their Godly character and future potential as quickly as he can and by doing so ultimately cripple the work of Christ in the earth.

As Daniel chapter one, verses three and four describe, Nebuchadnezzar first put emphasis on bringing *"certain"* of the children of Israel. He was very specific and selective concerning the type of youth he wanted. He didn't just want anybody. He didn't want to waste time with weeding out those youth who lacked potential and putting them in a class for special training. He wanted the best and the brightest, those who were quick learners, with razor sharp minds and meticulous perception.

Next Nebuchadnezzar said he wanted those *"in whom was no blemish"*. In other words, he wanted young people who hadn't been scarred physically or emotionally. He wanted those who had no negative behaviors. He wanted them pure, completely untainted.

The king also wanted children who were "*well favored*". He wanted the type of children whom everyone liked; children who are most likable typically are the ones others follow. They become leaders by virtue of the charisma they have that make others simply want to follow them. Nebuchadnezzar wanted this type of young person because of the influence they could exert over others.

Further, the young people Nebuchadnezzar chose had to be *"skillful in all wisdom, and cunning in knowledge, and understanding science"*. They had to be quick learners who exhibited maturity beyond their years. They had to be aware of history and the environment and had to have a firm grasp of science.

And lastly, but very significantly, they had to have an *"ability to stand in the king's palace"*. They had to look good. Their image and presence had to be profound. They had to be good speakers who could be put on an organizational chart as replacements for leaders in the kingdom of Babylon.

I believe the reason Nebuchadnezzar wanted the best and the brightest is because he thought it would be much easier and quicker for him to infuse or instill in them the ideologies of Babylon, without first having to go through the process of reprogramming them.

In a sense, Nebuchadnezzar could be considered the precursor to Adolph Hitler in that he desperately wanted to create a class of people that were shaped and molded totally into and after his wicked image. It seems he wanted to create the perfect, superior race, the race that would rule the world.

Chapter 6

Teach Your Children Well

*"And these words, which I command thee this day,
shall be in thine heart:
and thou shalt teach them diligently unto thy children. . ."*

~ Deuteronomy 6:6

King Nebuchadnezzar wanted to completely change the Hebrew boys he brought into captivity. He wanted to eradicate their Godly upbringing, their Israeli heritage and most of all their belief in their great God Jehovah.

And, that's what satan wants to do to today's young people, particularly those who were reared in a Godly, church-oriented environment. He wants to turn them into something completely different from what God wants them to be.

As previously noted, the fall of Adam and Eve plunged mankind into a sinful state. That's why in David's prayer in Psalm 51:5, he said *"Behold, I was shapen in iniquity and in sin did my mother conceive me"*.

This means that when a person is born, they are born with a nature to sin. Consequently, the only way for a person to get back into right relationship with God is to be changed from a sinner to a saint.

God sent his son Jesus to die for the sin's of the world and give us the opportunity to make that necessary change. That's the whole premise of the New Testament. It's about change.

God wants to change our nature from that which was made after Adam (the Adamic, sinful nature) into that which is made after Christ (holy and pure). That's why Paul said in II Corinthians 5:17 *"if any man be in Christ, he is a new creature, old things are passed away and behold, all things are become new"*.

This change Paul is describing has to do with a person's character, their inner self, how they think and carry themselves. It has to do with how they respond to the circumstances of life. In effect, Paul is describing a recreation or rebirth process in which a person's former sinful nature or character is transformed into a nature or character that is a reflection of God's holy nature.

Paul reiterated this Biblical concept of change in Ephesians chapter 4, verses 22 through 24. It states *"that ye put off concerning the former conversation the old man, which is corrupt according to the deceitful lusts; and be renewed in the spirit of your mind; and that ye put on the new man, which after God is created in righteousness and true holiness"*.

For further clarification, Paul said in Romans 8:29 *"for whom he did foreknow, he also did predestinate to be conformed to the image of his Son, that he might be the firstborn among many brethren"*.

Simply put, God wants us to take on the nature of Christ or become like Christ or like as Christ.

While God certainly gives us the wherewithal to make that transformation through reception of the Holy Spirit, the big problem is the devil tries everything in his power to reverse the transformation process. He is wholly motivated to make us into the exact opposite of what God wants us to be and that is after his wicked and self-motivated persona.

Satan goes about doing this the very same way Nebuchadnezzar did in trying to change the nature of the young Israelis. The book of Daniel describes how after the king deported them to Babylon, he immediately set about to change them from what they were. He wanted to rid them of the Godly upbringing, the Biblical teachings and the spiritual roots their parents and community leaders had instilled in them from birth.

Let me point out here, a Biblical parenting principle. God mandated that the people of Israel teach their children the principles of God from the day they were born. They were to saturate their minds and souls with the Word of God by putting the Word as frontlets (a band) on their foreheads, by writing it upon doorposts and by posting it upon the walls of their homes and their schools. Everywhere the children went, they would inevitably be exposed to and reminded about the eternal Word of God.

"And these words, which I command thee this day, shall be in thine heart: and thou shalt teach them diligently unto thy children, and shalt

Chapter 5: Satan Wants To Get 'Em In Their Prime

talk of them when thou sittest in thine house, and when thou walkest by the way, and when thou liest down, and when thou risest up.

"And, thou shalt bind them for a sign upon thine hand, and they shall be as frontlets between thine eyes.

"And thou shalt write them upon the posts of thy house, and on thy gates." (Deuteronomy 6:6-9)

One of the biggest and most fatal mistakes many modern day parents tend to make is that of neglecting to baptize or saturate their children in and with the Word of God by not only exposing them to it in church, but by showering them with it in the homes.

What I mean by this is that many parents often do not take their children to church on a regular basis, nor do they discuss the Word of God with them around the house or in other one-on-one conversations.

Parents are afraid of rebellion

I believe one reason parents don't do this is they're afraid that requiring their children to be in church "too much" will cause them to rebel when they get older and stop going to church altogether. They're afraid that if they talk about God too much around the house, the child will accuse them of always preaching to them and stop the lines of communication.

The sad part of all this is that it has happened and continues to happen far too often. There are many cases I'm personally familiar with in which parents have been so strict when it comes to their children's church attendance and their so-called "Godly" rules around the home that their children have completely rebelled and turned their backs on God.

No Christian family is immune from this potential situation, including pastors and ministers. I know of a situation in which the sons of a pastor and wife had become so defiant that they openly boasted about storing drugs and weapons inside their home and didn't care what their parents thought about it.

On the other end of the spectrum is when parents do all the "right things" regarding rearing their children in a Holy, Christian environment, but then the children still wander away from their church upbringing.

It's definitely difficult to accept when you've done all you know to do and your child still decides to live his or her life outside of Christ. It's hard seeing a child of yours struggle trying to make it in life and go through hard trials unnecessarily because of breaking their relationship with God.

Worst yet, it sometimes results in tragedy.

That's why 1 Peter 5:8 warns us about satan, the lion, who's trying to rob us of our lives and souls, as we discussed in Chapter 1. Again, it says to "*be sober, be vigilant; because your adversary the devil, as a roaring lion walketh about, seeking whom he may devour*".

I was completely floored the first time I encountered satan's ultimate wrath. At that time, I was young in the Lord. I was very idealistic when it came to serving God, and didn't understand that bad things actually happened to saints.

In this case, it involved the pastor of the church I attended during the time I was a graduate student pursuing a master's degree. It was also during the early years of my newly found walk with God.

The pastor had a son who was around 16 at the time I attended the church. The son was bright, good-looking and an excellent drummer. I didn't know much about the son so was unaware of any struggles he may have been having regarding his relationship with God.

However, he later stopped attending church and started running the streets. I was informed several years later, that he got shot. He was seriously injured but survived the subsequent surgeries and was soon released from the hospital to go home. But one day while his parents were away from home, he had some complications from his injuries and died.

While that terrible situation happened many years ago, another hit more recently and more closely to home. A friend of mine had twin boys. They are the same age as my oldest son and played with him on the same city champion midget football team when they were nine and ten years old. One later played on the high school's state championship football team in my hometown.

My friend was very diligent in rearing his sons in a Christian manner. He'd lived in the streets for many years before becoming a Christian and did all he could to protect his sons from them. He knew what lurked in the streets. He knew about the drugs, the alcohol, and the death.

Chapter 5: Satan Wants To Get 'Em In Their Prime

He kept his boys involved in church, sports and other positive activities. He took them to the gym to work on their basketball and other athletic skills. He was at their practices. He didn't miss their games. He talked with them. He counseled with them. He became their friend and protector.

My friend was like me in this regard. He gave his life to his sons out of the love he had for them.

That's why it hurt so much the morning I heard the news that one of the twins had been shot and killed. It was a tragic loss. The son, even at the young age of 22, had opened up his own business. He was running a clothing store inside the local mall. He was on his way to doing well for himself, to becoming a business leader in the community – until calamity struck late one night.

Several men knocked on his back door around midnight. He went out to talk with them. According to news reports, a dispute ensued over drugs and money. One of the men pulled a gun and shot him in the chest. My friend's son staggered back into his kitchen, and then fell dead.

When I got the news, a dagger went through my heart. It was like one of my sons had been killed. I can imagine what my friend must have thought during that turbulent time. "How did this happen when I invested so much time, so much energy and so many prayers into protecting this boy? Where did I go wrong?"

The fact of the matter is, what happened to his son wasn't his fault. It wasn't anything he did wrong. It couldn't be attributed to anything he neglected to do. The fact is that his son was a grown man and apparently made some bad decisions, despite seemingly being on a positive track.

Another example involved a friend from a church we attended in another Ohio city. My wife received a call from her best friend. A mutual friend of theirs had just been notified that her 25-year-old son who'd been missing 17 days had been found. But sadly, he was discovered dead of two gunshot wounds to his body.

The son, who still holds the basketball scoring record at the high school he attended, had moved away to a bigger city. He didn't continue living according to the Godly principles he'd been taught and got involved in some dangerous things that cost him his life.

Was it the mother's fault? Not at all. She had done all she could to raise her son in the fear of God. In fact, he attended Sunday School and church with my sons. It was his decision to move away and get involved in what he had. There was nothing she could have done, other than pray for God's divine protection.

Did she trust God to keep her son? I'm sure she did. So why did God allow such a horrible thing to happen? Again, God is the one who makes the ultimate decision on whether a person lives or dies.

"See now that I, even I, am he, and there is no god with me: I kill, and I make alive; I wound and I heal: neither is there any that can deliver out of my hand." (Deuteronomy 32:39)

The last example I'll give is the story of another good friend of mine who was an excellent singer and sang in a gospel singing group that I put together concerts for. One of his sons, again raised in a Christian home, chose to leave his teachings and get involved in drugs and people who dealt in drugs.

The end result was the son had his life taken by a drug dealer's gun at the way too young age of 27.

I know other parents that I've attended church with and am good friends with whose children have grown up and left their Christian upbringings. Thank God, not all have gotten involved in drugs or some other criminal activity which cost them their lives, but they've still gotten themselves in difficult circumstances as a result of the choice they made to leave God.

The truth is that when people—young or old—turn their backs on God and begin engaging in sin, they put themselves in a position in which God will leave them to their own devices.

Romans 1:21, states that *"...when they knew God, they glorified him not as God, neither were thankful; but became vain in their imaginations and their foolish heart was darkened"*.

As a result, according to Romans 1:28 God will *"give them over to a reprobate mind to do those things that are not convenient"*. Sadly and

Chapter 5: Satan Wants To Get 'Em In Their Prime

tragically, what this does is leave the person outside the "arc of safety" God had them in. They forfeit His protection. It leaves them in a vulnerable place where the devil can launch an all-out attack against them, without God being there to defend them.

One pervasive problem that exists with young people is they're often prone to putting themselves at risk. They think their youth gives them immunity from malady. But just like anything else, when you expose yourself to fire often enough, eventually you're going to get burned.

I like to use the simple example of driving an automobile. Many of us make a habit of exceeding the official speed limit. We've heard that most law enforcement officers typically allow a five to 10 mile per hour grace in which they won't ticket you for speeding. But, if they want to, they legally have every right to do so.

So if you make a habit of driving five to 10 miles per hour over the posted speed limit, you shouldn't get upset if you're stopped and ticketed.

However, the problem many people have is they often increase their risk or exposure. They'll drive 10 to 20 miles per hour over the limit, thereby increasing their risk. They may get by for a while, but sooner or later, they'll suffer the consequences of maximizing their risk.

As tough as it is, despite the tears we have to shed, the heartache we have to endure, we still have to accept the immutable fact that God is sovereign and that He still gives everyone free will or free choice. While it's His will that we all choose Him, far too often people choose to go their own way without Him, despite the potential consequences.

Nebuchadnezzar Is After My Child

Chapter 7

How Far Do We Go?

"Neither give place to the devil."

~ Ephesians 4:27

Knowing how far to go when it comes to balancing your child's "church" life with their every day living is definitely a dilemma many parents have found themselves with. Balance is the key word.

I'm a strong advocate that Christian parents have to provide their children a good balance between their church activities and those outside of the church. And it requires being very prayerful and spirit-led to pull it off successfully.

While parents in the "old days" were well meaning, many typically did not allow their children to attend sporting events, movie theaters, school dances and many other social activities. They simply forbade these types of activities across the board because they saw them as wicked and sinful and as they so unequivocally quoted *"the Bible says to 'come out from among them and be ye separate'"*. (II Corinthians 6:17)

My mother was that type of saved parent. She got saved when I was in fourth grade. Prior to that, there weren't many rules in our house. We could run the streets at random, listen to secular radio in the house, dance with the kids on Dick Clark's American Bandstand and go to the movies.

But afterwards, all this freedom was taken away. Things at home became extremely strict. We couldn't watch American Bandstand or listen to the "blues" on the radio. My mother viewed it as sin.

My older siblings, whom my mother couldn't control, continued doing their thing. The younger ones, starting with me, since I was still young enough to control, were confined to the house and backyard. Home became like a prison that we couldn't wait to be released from.

That's why, as I wrote about in my autobiography, as soon as I turned 14 years old, I hit the streets with abandon.

Granted, there are many activities that if properly screened and/or chaperoned are wholesome enough for children of saved parents to participate in. But the prevailing attitude was and sometimes is today to prohibit anything that comes close to looking like sin or promoting sinful behavior.

But like a friend of mine, who now is a successful gospel artist, told my wife and me during a chance meeting in a mall, the first time he went to a theater after becoming an adult, he was shocked that going to movies had been considered taboo. He didn't see sin running rampant in the building and was perplexed at what the older generation had been so concerned about.

Yes, he understood there were R or X-rated movies being shown on some screens. And, he knew these were to be avoided. He attended a family-oriented movie.

It's that discretion that many older, saved parents didn't allow room for. They broad-brushed all movie-going as sin.

When it comes to watching movies in theaters or on television, most Christians clearly understand the danger of participating in or viewing lewd or sexually explicit images. However, many aren't so clear about the importance of not viewing other practices that *"give place to the devil"* (Ephesians 4:27), such as participating in witchcraft, magic or fortune-telling. These activities are some of the most popular subjects in today's movie and television industries.

Have you noticed the glut of movies that have been made in recent years that glorify the devil? They portray him as one that has all power and one that in many cases is all right to worship and to follow.

This type of movie genre got kick-started with the popularity of "The Exorcist", which first was released by Warner Brothers in 1973.

Since then, there has been a string of movies that glorify and popularize the devil, with the Harry Potter movie franchise being one of the more recent and tremendously popular.

Chapter 7: How Far Do We Go?

The movies are based on the Harry Potter book series. According to Wikipedia, the novels chronicle the life of a young wizard[1], Harry Potter[2], and his friends Hermione Granger[3] and Ron Weasley[4], all of whom are students at Hogwarts School of Witchcraft and Wizardry[5].

The main premise of the books concern Harry's struggle against Lord Voldemort[6], the Dark wizard who intends to become immortal, overthrow the Ministry of Magic, subjugate non-magic people and destroy anyone who stands in his way.

Wikipedia reported in 2016 that without inflation adjustment, the Harry Potter movie series was the second highest-grossing film series[7] with $7.7 billion in worldwide receipts, of which seven out of eight films are among the 50 highest-grossing films[8].

While many non-believers and, sadly, increasing numbers of believers contend the Harry Potter movies and books are just innocent entertainment, the movies contain a dangerous and wicked message. They glorify and promote the sin of witchcraft, a practice that stems directly from the pit of hell, and something God emphatically tells us to avoid.

"When thou art come into the land which the Lord thy God giveth thee, thou shalt not learn to do after the abomination of those nations.

"There shall not be found among you any one that taketh his son or his daughter to pass through the fire, or that useth divination, or an observer of times, or an enchanter, or a witch,

"Or a charmer, or a consulter with familiar spirits, or a wizard, or a necromancer (a person who conjures up spirits of the dead for the purpose of revealing the future or influencing the course of events).

"For all these things are an abomination unto the Lord:" (Deuteronomy 18:9-12).

Witches, wizards, magicians, fortune tellers. They're abominations to God and if young people are to survive the onslaught of satan, they need to stay as far away from them as possible.

To thine own self be true

One of my personal practices has been a refusal to watch movies that glorify the devil. Personally, I feel that the world is giving enough glory to satan than for me to consciously watch in my home or pay money to see a movie that sets him up as bigger than God.

On the other hand, what might be all right for one person to view may not be all right for another person. It all depends on a person's tolerance and maturity level.

For example, some people can't handle viewing a simple kissing scene without getting sexually aroused, or viewing a scene where the actors are drinking or doing drugs without being tempted to sin themselves.

In these cases, it's important to "know thyself". As the renowned poet William Shakespeare so eloquently penned in his famous play Hamlet: *"This above all: to thine own self be true, And it must follow, as the night the day, Thou canst not then be false to any man."*

Everyone has to know what they personally are able to handle to avoid putting themselves in a position where they might succumb to sinning.

The point here is, if adults can be challenged by the tantalizing things we get exposed to, it only stands to reason that young people are likewise challenged. Add in the fact their hormones are raging in their teens and early twenties, it can be a recipe for disaster.

Why can't we just be real and admit that some things have the potential to bother us. No, it doesn't mean that we're any less a Saint. It simply means we're human. If certain things arouse our flesh, then we need to learn how to keep ourselves away from them.

Remember what the Bible says about the flesh? Here are a couple examples.

The Apostle Paul said in Romans 7:18 *"for I know that in me (that is in my flesh) dwelleth no good thing: for to will is present with me; but how to perform that which is good I find not".*

Paul also taught in 1 Corinthians 9:27 about the importance of keeping our bodies under subjection or control. He said, *"But I keep under my body, and bring it into subjection: lest that by any means, when I have preached to others, I myself should be a castaway."*

And how about what John said in I John 2:16: *"For all that is in the world, the lust of the flesh, and the lust of the eyes, and the pride of life, is not of the Father, but is of the world".*

Chapter 7: How Far Do We Go?

The lust of the eyes or going after something that appealed to the sight is what got King David in trouble.

"And it came to pass in an evening tide, that David arose from off his bed, and walked upon the roof of the king's house: and from the roof he saw a woman washing herself; and the woman was very beautiful to look upon. And David sent and inquired after the woman. And one said, is not this Bathsheba, the daughter of Eliam, the wife of Uriah the Hittite? And David sent messengers, and took her, and she came in unto him, and he lay with her. . ." (II Samuel 11:2, 3)

The rest is a history lesson all of us should take note of. David got himself in immense trouble with God for giving in to the whims of his flesh, starting with his seeing a beautiful woman. After Bathsheba became pregnant, he immediately tried to cover up his sin. You know what it's like to try to cover up a wrong. One wrong leads to another, and another and another.

David's sin with Bathsheba eventually led him to murdering her husband, Uriah, by ordering that he be sent to the front lines of battle. It later caused him to lie to the prophet Nathan about stealing *"the poor man's lamb"* (II Samuel 12:4-6).

But the worst thing of all, is that you will always have to pay dearly for the sin you commit. In David's case, it led to the heart-wrenching death of his child that was born of Bathsheba.

That's why it is so important we take heed to the scripture that declares *"the wages of sin is death".* (Romans 6:23)

Come out from among them

Having raised three children and now a grandfather, I get the reasoning behind the older generation forbidding young people from participating in secular activities they believed were sinful. They were doing their best to protect their young from satan's attacks against their natural inclinations and vulnerabilities.

And, I totally agree with the Biblical principle that instructs us to *"come out from among them and be ye separate"* (Romans 12:1). But I also believe the ability to do that has to start with the proper mindset.

We have to recognize that while all things may be lawful, all things aren't expedient to do. So we have to learn how to use discretion regarding the things we allow our children to be exposed to. And, we have to instill that type of mindset in them.

Young people also must understand that how they think in their minds must be the separating factor when it comes to sin. God doesn't want us to be of the same mind as those outside his Heavenly realm. Rather, he said" *a carnal mind is enmity (actively opposed to) against God"*.

Paul added in Philippians 2:6, that we should *"let this mind be in you, which was also in Christ Jesus"*. That's a mindset that's focused on God and refers to how Jesus' sole purpose was to please God, his father. As Jesus declared in John 4:34: *"My meat (purpose/mission) is to do the will of him that sent me, and to finish his work"*.

So that's where the real separation comes into play.

Chapter 8

Change Their Nature

"Whom they might teach the learning and the tongue of the Chaldeans"

~ *Daniel 1:4*

The sad result of not exposing young people to God's Word is we now have a generation or more of youth who largely have no consciousness toward God. When it comes to doing wrong, they don't have that inner voice to tell them it's not right. They're ruled by their minds and by what they've learned in the society they live in that tells them it's alright to do what you feel like doing—as long as it doesn't hurt anybody else. Their consciences have truly been *"seared with a hot iron"*. (I Timothy 4:2)

This is a trap that young people and older people often fall into—believing that things are right just because they decide that it's right in their minds, even though it may be contrary to what God's Word says.

The great wise man, Solomon, characterized it this way in Proverbs 14:12: *"There is a way which seemeth right unto a man, but the end thereof are the ways of death"*.

A person doing what he or she "thinks" is right also is similar to the time of the judges when the Israelites ignored the Holy standards God had set for them. During that time, the Israelites gave no regard for what God wanted and the guidelines he had set for their lives. Rather, according to Judges 21:25, *"in those days there was no king in Israel: every man did that which was right in his own eyes"*.

This scriptural passage further points out the importance of the need for good parenting when it comes to teaching children the Word of God, so it can be their compass for doing what is right. Without that compass, they will determine within themselves "what is right".

I believe strongly that the only thing that kept me from falling completely off the cliff when I was young and before I was saved was the moral compass or God consciousness that had been imparted in me during the years my mother made us go to Sunday School.

Yes, I said she **made** us go to Sunday School. We didn't like it and stopped going as soon as we were too old for her to make us go anymore. But, the Biblical teaching I received during those early years in my life paid off in immense dividends. It put a fear and reverence toward God within me that never went away.

Consequently, despite the depth of sin that I descended to, there was still enough God consciousness in me that it gave me at least some degree of restraint. When it came to sin, I would only go so far. There always seemed to be a voice inside speaking to me about not going all the way, about not crossing the threshold into complete oblivion.

Lack of consciousness

On the other hand, many friends of mine and other young people I grew up with who hadn't been brought up in church didn't have the same harness that I seemed to have. I saw them have no fear or reservations at all about fighting to hurt someone else or doing other wrongs. They didn't care. They had no God consciousness that worked restraint in them. Consequently, they were easy prey for the devil to enslave and become the mastermind of their destiny.

That's exactly what Nebuchadnezzar wanted to do with the young Hebrew boys. He wanted to eliminate their God consciousness by teaching them *"the tongue of the Chaldeans"*. Chaldea was the country of which Babylon was the capital.

In teaching the young Hebrews the *"tongue"* or language and practices of the Chaldeans, Nebuchadnezzar, in effect, would be teaching them the ways, the conversation, the style, the culture and behavior of the Chaldeans. His ultimate goal was to "make them into" Chaldeans, so much so that when you looked at them you'd never know they originally came from Judah.

I'm sure many of you have experienced seeing someone for the first time in many years. It was a person you'd known from years before. It could have been a friend or the son or daughter of a friend.

Chapter 8: Change Their Nature

They tried their best to make you remember where you knew them from, but they looked and acted so differently from what you remembered. You couldn't believe it was actually the person you knew before. They had become somebody you just didn't recognize.

What happened is that they'd gone away from their upbringing and exposed themselves to an environment that made them into something else, something strange, something totally different than what they were raised up to be.

This can also happen in much less dramatic fashion. Parents can find themselves hardly or not at all recognizing their own children because they've allowed them to so conform to the trends and fads of the world that they end up losing a sense of who they are.

Think about those youth with spiked hair containing green, red or pink tints; those youth with dreadlocks shielding nearly their entire faces. What about those youth who have tattoos painting nearly their entire bodies, or earrings hanging from noses or other body parts. And how about those who wear such outlandish clothing that changes their natural appearance altogether.

Now before you jump on me, I don't object to fashion trends and looking good. I understand that clothing and hair styles change. After all, I grew up during the era when Afro hair-styles came into vogue. The style was considered extremely radical at the time, but today is called a natural style and worn by people of all races.

Dressing to be Super Fly

What I do have a problem with is when the fashion or style of the day goes to the outer limits. When the fashion takes over the personality of the child and the child ends up living out a fantasy based on the fashion.

I did it myself in the 70's. If you're a baby boomer who grew up during the late sixties and seventies, you probably did it to.

Are you old enough to remember the Super Fly and Shaft movies that popularized wide-brimmed gangster hats, long, flowing coats and platform shoes? I got caught up in this style of dress, but worst than that; I got caught up in the "attitude" of the style of dress.

Not only was I dressing to "be like" Super Fly, I was dressing "to be" Super Fly. And as a result, I lost the person whom I was and became someone I was not. In my mind, I was this super-cool guy who dealt in drugs, didn't like "the man" and had a plan to get rich and go off into the sunset. But in reality, I was a young, naive guy who knew very little about life and what it took to be successful.

What about you? What movie character did you become? What singer did you emulate? Who did you lose your identify for? Most of us have been there and done that.

This tactic of changing the character of young people has been a tactic of the devil throughout the ages. When Nebuchadnezzar employed it with the Hebrew boys, it wasn't a new thing. It actually was a spinoff of the genocidal attempt made by the king of Egypt to kill all the young men of Israel, as recorded in the first chapter of the book of Exodus.

But in order to understand what happened there, we first have to look at what happened with a young man named Joseph and how satan unleashed an all-out attack to destroy him.

Part II

The Thief Cometh To Kill!

Chapter 9

Satan Wants To Kill Your Dreams

"What happens to a dream deferred?
Does it dry up, like a raisin in the sun?
Or fester like a sore – and then run?
Does it stink like rotten meat?
Or crust and sugar over – like a syrupy sweet?
Maybe it just sags, like a heavy load.
Or does it explode?"

~ Langston Hughes

The story of Joseph begins in the book of Genesis, chapters 37-50. The story illustrates how God is able to rescue His people from the pit of despair and elevate them to positions of power and authority. But, it's also a story of how satan despises young dreamers and his unrelenting attempts to kill their dreams.

Joseph was the second youngest of the 12 sons of Jacob. At an early age, Joseph had a very deep consciousness toward and intimate relationship with God. As a result of Joseph's intense relationship with God, God allowed him to have visions and dreams that reached far beyond the imagination of his brothers. God showed him that he would be a ruler over many and that even his brothers would show obeisance or servitude to him.

As it is with most big brothers, they don't like it when a younger brother talks in a manner that makes them think he's better than they are. Consequently, the older brothers plotted to put Joseph in his place. Initially, they planned to do away with him altogether by taking his life.

But after Reuben, the oldest brother, thought about the serious consequences of murdering their brother, he convinced the others to sell Joseph to a group of Ishmeelite traders. These traders took Joseph to

Egypt and then sold him to Potiphar, Pharaoh's captain of the guard. You can find the story in Genesis chapters 37 and 38.

Joseph was only 17 when he was taken to Egypt, away from the safety of his homeland, his family and his Godly culture. You can imagine the trauma this must have caused him.

But worst of all, being sold into Egypt effectively meant that Joseph was sold into slavery. He literally became a slave to the regime of Pharaoh. Along with his freedom, all his rights and privileges were taken away and he was obligated to be obedient to his "master", which is exactly the position satan wants to put young people in today.

Webster's dictionary defines slavery as "the state of being subject to a master; lack of liberty to do as one pleases, specifically lack of freedom to determine one's course of action and conditions of living."

Slavery further implies subjection to a master who owns ones person and may treat one as property. It implies a state of being bound in law or by physical restraint to a state of complete subjection to the will of another.

Simply put, Joseph was stripped of his identity. The only thing he had left was his unwavering belief and faith in Jehovah God. And, it was that faith and belief which God honored.

Joseph was assigned to work in the house of his master, Potiphar, and found favor with him. Potiphar noticed that the Lord was with Joseph and caused everything he did to prosper. Potiphar's house was also blessed for Joseph's sake. As a result, Potiphar ultimately elevated Joseph to overseer of his house and over all that he had. (Genesis: 39:2-6)

But Joseph was still a slave and as such, it didn't take long for satan to rear his ugly head. Joseph would soon face a formidable test in which he'd have to make a stand for God that potentially could cost him his life.

Shortly after Potiphar promoted Joseph to overseer of his house, satan used Potiphar's wife in a brazen attempt to destroy him. She "*cast her eyes upon Joseph; and she said, Lie with me.*" (Genesis 39:7b)

But Joseph never wavered from his loyalty to God and to his master. He refused the sexual advances the woman made day after day. He didn't

Chapter 9: Satan Wants To Kill Your Dreams

toy with her requests. He didn't fantasize about being with her. He simply stood his ground as a true man of God should.

He gallantly declared: *". . . Behold, my master wotteth not what is with me in the house, and he hath committed all that he hath to my hand; There is none greater in this house than I; neither hath he kept back anything from me but thee, because thou art his wife: how then can I do this great wickedness, and sin against God?"* (Genesis 39:8-9)

That really made the devil furious. He consequently influenced Potiphar's wife to be even more aggressive in her pursuit of getting Joseph to commit sin with her. One day while passing him, she caught him by his garment in a attempt to force him to give in.

But Joseph fled her clutches, unfortunately, leaving his garment dangling in her hand. Seizing the opportunity, she called out to the men of her house and lied that Joseph had tried to have sex with her.

And when she told her husband, Potiphar, he had no choice but to put Joseph *". . into the prison, a place where the king's prisoners were bound:"* (Genesis 39:20)

From the pit to the palace

Even though the situation looked bleak and desperate to Joseph, God never forgot the dreamer nor his dreams, and he came to his rescue. Despite having to endure the false accusation lodged by Potiphar's wife and undeserved imprisonment, Joseph continued to remain loyal to God, and God remained loyal to him.

Genesis chapter 40 tells the story of how the Pharaoh later was offended by his butler and his baker. Pharaoh got so angry that he put the butler and baker into prison—the same ward where young Joseph was bound.

Not long afterwards, the butler and baker dreamed dreams which God allowed Joseph to interpret. The baker's dream meant that he'd soon be killed. The butler's dream meant that he'd soon be restored to his former position with Pharaoh; and Joseph asked that when this happened if he'd repay him by mentioning him to Pharaoh to bring him also out of prison.

But, as the devil would have it, while Joseph's interpretations came true, the butler selfishly forgot to mention Joseph to the king—until two years later—as it's recorded in Genesis 41.

That's when the Pharaoh had two dreams that no one could interpret. The butler, then, finally remembered Joseph and told Pharaoh about how he had interpreted his dream.

Pharaoh immediately sent his guards to bring Joseph to him out of the dungeon and said to him *"I have heard say of thee, that thou canst understand a dream to interpret it. And Joseph answered, It is not me: God shall give Pharaoh an answer of peace".*

To summarize, God gave Joseph the interpretation of the dream, and he related it to Pharaoh.

"And the thing was good in the eyes of Pharaoh, and in the eyes of all his servants. And Pharaoh said unto his servants, Can we find such a one as this is, a man in whom the Spirit of God is? And Pharaoh said unto Joseph, Forasmuch as God hath shewed thee all this, there is none so discreet and wise as thou art:

"Thou shalt be over my house, and according unto thy word shall all my people be ruled: only in the throne will I be greater than thou." (Genesis 41:37-40)

There's a saying we have in church: "He may not come when you want him, but he's always right on time"

That's exactly what Joseph learned. While he desperately wanted the baker to remember him when he first was released from prison, the man let him down. Joseph subsequently had to suffer imprisonment for two more long years. But, even though the baker initially forgot Joseph, God never did and ultimately came to his rescue as a result of Pharaoh having his dreams.

The key is that Joseph never compromised his convictions regarding God. In spite of his disappointment, he stood firm in his God and waited on Him to come through. It's a lesson all young people need to take heed to, no matter what the challenge or test. Stay true to God, and God will stay true to you.

Chapter 9: Satan Wants To Kill Your Dreams

The ultimate result of Joseph's stand was that when a famine later gripped the land, he was able to reunite with his family, reconcile with his brothers and save the entire nation of Israel from starvation and ultimate death.

Yes, Joseph's brothers had despised him as a dreamer, and Satan used them in an attempt to destroy Joseph. It was a situation that looked hopeless and Joseph could have despaired of life and turned his back on God.

But, the lesson he learned and something all young people should take heart in is that God will sometimes take a situation that man means for bad, and turn it completely around for not only our good, but for the good of our entire family. And, in Joseph's case, it was good for the entire nation of Israel.

"And Pharaoh spake unto Joseph, saying, Thy father and thy brethren are come unto thee: The land of Egypt is before thee; in the best of the land make thy father and brethren to dwell; in the land of Goshen let them dwell: and if thou knowest any men of activity among them, then make them rulers over my cattle." (Genesis 47:5-6)

Joseph's story is a clear representation of how the devil tries his best to bring youth into a state of slavery or bondage, where he takes complete authority or control over them. He wants to become their master, the puppeteer who manipulates their every action.

When he says go, they go. When he says come, they come. He has total control of their will so much so that they can't even see what they're doing themselves.

When it gets to this point, that's when it's so difficult for parents to exert any influence over their children at all. It has become an all-out battle between the parent and satan himself. On one hand, the parent is doing all he or she can to influence their child in the right way. On the other hand, satan is not only whispering in the child's mind, he's loudly screaming his directions regarding what he wants them to do and how he wants them to live.

The sad result in far too many cases is that satan wins out and ultimately leads our young people down a dark road to destruction. He ultimately accomplishes his goal of stealing their dreams, killing their futures and destroying their souls.

Remember the scripture that was quoted earlier *"the thief (satan) cometh not but for to steal, kill and destroy"*. Joseph's story gives a clear example of satan's strategy to do that by killing dreams, goals and aspirations.

Dreams, goals and aspirations are the important elements that motivate us and drive us forward in life. The man, woman, boy or girl who doesn't have dreams, goals or aspirations doesn't have much of a life. They have nothing to push them forward with and they end up stuck in a place they don't want to be, a place of frustration and loneliness.

On the other hand, when you have the tenacity to hold onto your goals and dreams, God will always come through for you. When you refuse to allow the tests and temptations of the devil to rob you of your desire to be better and have more in life, your darkness will invariably turn to light. The day will always break. The sun will always shine. Just like it did with Joseph.

Chapter 10

Who Is Your God?

"And if it seem evil unto you to serve the Lord, choose you this day whom ye will serve;"

~ Joshua 24:15a

Joseph's story is a great example of what God will do in a young person's life when they hold on to him. He will give you victory out of the jaws of defeat.

But when you live for God, most of us have learned that after major victories come major tests. And that's what happened with Joseph and later the children of Israel. After the death of the Pharaoh who had befriended Joseph and promoted him in the kingdom, the Bible records that *"there arose up a new king over Egypt, which knew not Joseph"*. (Exodus 1:8)

This Pharaoh, according to Exodus 1:9, immediately became either jealous or intimidated over the fact that *"the people of the children of Israel are more and mightier than we"*. So he quickly launched a plan to destroy the nation by wiping out the sons.

"Come on," he said, *"let us deal wisely with them; lest they multiply, and it come to pass, that, when there falleth out any war, they join also unto our enemies, and fight against us, and so get them up out of the land"*. (Exodus 1:10)

This new king's first attempt at destroying the nation of Israel was setting taskmasters over the people to afflict them with heavy burdens. But the more they afflicted them, the more they multiplied and grew. The more the nation grew, the more the Egyptians afflicted them.

"And the Egyptians made the children of Israel to serve with rigor. They made their lives bitter with hard bondage, in mortar, and in brick,

and in all manner of service in the field: all their service, wherein they made them serve, was with rigor". (Exodus 1:14)

But it didn't work, and the king of Egypt had to take the ultimate step. He first spoke to the Hebrew midwives and ordered them to kill all the newborn male babies. But this plan didn't work either because *"the midwives feared God, and did not as the king of Egypt commanded"* (Exodus 1:17). And the nation of Israel continued to multiply.

Of course this infuriated the Pharaoh and as a last resort, he ordered his soldiers to throw every newborn son of the Israelites into the raging river. Can you imagine the cries and moans of the mothers and fathers as the soldiers burst into their homes, snatched their babies out of their cribs or out of their laps and carried them down to the river?

Can you imagine the anguish and heartbreak the mothers and fathers must have felt hearing the screams of their babies and the splashing of the water as they were tossed in the river with no chance of survival?

The whole purpose behind Pharaoh killing the sons of Egypt was to maintain control over the people. He knew that the strength and future of the nation of Israel resided in the loins of the sons and in order for him to maintain rulership over the nation, the sons had to be destroyed.

As we know, God has and will always protect His chosen people. Despite the king's edict to throw all the sons into the river, God delivered the baby named Moses when his mother hid him three months and then put him in an ark of bulrushes on the banks of the river where he was found by Pharaoh's daughter. Subsequently, Moses was raised in the palace of the king who had wanted him dead. And, of course, Moses, went on to be the one God chose to lead His people out of Egypt.

But, one irrefutable fact about satan is that defeats don't stop him from his pursuit to destroy people. He never gives up. He's relentless. He's tenacious. This is quite evident in the fact that despite God using Joseph, and later Moses, to deliver the children of Israel out of the hand of the Pharaohs, satan subsequently went after the younger generation of Israelites.

Look what happened just a few years after the nation of Israel had been delivered out of Egyptian bondage. It was after Moses and Joshua had

Chapter 10: Who Is Your God?

died. The report is found in the book of Judges, chapter 2, beginning at verse 8.

"And Joshua the son of Nun the servant of the Lord, died, being an hundred and ten years old. And they buried him in the border of his inheritance in Timnatheres, in the mount of Ephraim on the north side of the hill Gaash.

"And also all that generation were gathered unto their fathers: and there arose another generation after them, which knew not the Lord, nor yet the works which he had done for Israel.

"And they forsook the Lord God of their fathers, which brought them out of the land of Egypt, and followed other gods, of the gods of the people that were round about them, and bowed themselves unto them, and provoked the Lord to anger. And they forsook the Lord, and served Baal and Ashtaroth."

Gods that can't see

Baal typically referred to the farm god of the Phoenicians and Canaanites. He was reputedly responsible for crops, flocks and fecund (fruitful) farm families. Each locality had its own Baal. The Baalim (many Baals) were worshiped on high places with lascivious (lustful, lewd) rites, self-torture and human sacrifice.

On the other hand, Ashtaroth is plural for Ashtoreth, the name of any of the fertility goddesses of the ancient Near East. And listen to this, the historian Gensenius related the name Ashtoreth to the Persian word "sitarah" or "star" and connects it with Venus, the goddess of love.

Baal and Ashtoreth. Think about and look at how satan systematically lures our young to the dark side. Rather than worship the God they had been taught about, the youthful generation of Israel preferred being like the world. They preferred following after the false gods of the world like Baal and Ashtoreth.

It's simple if you don't get it. Satan lured the younger generation of Israel away from the true and living God to the gods who represented material possessions, false religious rites and deviant sexual behavior. It's like Paul related in I Corinthians 10:7, *"the people sat down to eat and drink, then rose up to play"*.

An example of this type of mentality is the rich farmer described in the book of Luke, chapter 12, verses 16 through 21. *"And he (Jesus) spake a parable unto them, saying, the ground of a certain rich man brought forth plentifully: and he thought within himself, saying, what shall I do, because I have no room where to bestow my fruits?*

" And he said, This will I do: I will pull down my barns, and build greater, and there will I bestow all my fruits and my goods, and I will say to my soul, Soul, thou hast much goods laid up for many years: take thine ease, eat, drink and be merry".

This is the prevailing attitude of far too many young people in our society today who only want to accumulate material possessions and let the good times roll. Yet, they fail to take the time to consider their eternal destination. The sad result of the rich farmer's way of thinking is found in verses 20 and 21.

"But God said unto him, Thou fool, this night thy soul shall be required of thee: then whose shall those things be, which thou has provided. So is he that layeth up treasure for himself, and is not rich toward God."

It goes without saying that the nation of Israel immediately began a downward spiral in morals and values and everything that God had done for them was unnecessarily negated. If you follow through the book of Judges, you'll see clearly the futility of the Israeli people when they tried to live without God on their side.

Time after time after time, they did the wrong thing and fell into the hands of the enemy. They became slaves to those out for nothing but to utterly change who they were and ultimately destroy them.

That's exactly what the devil wants and precisely what Nebuchadnezzar wanted to happen through his attack on the young Hebrew hostages.

Chapter 11

Do I Know You?

". . . we wept, when we remembered Zion . . ."

~ Psalms 137:1

Let's take a look now at the tactics satan used in his attack to change the nature of the Hebrew boys. The book of Daniel chapter 1, verses three through five reveal what they are, through the example of what King Nebuchadnezzar did. First, he ordered that they be removed from their familiar surroundings. In verse three he commanded his soldiers to *"bring certain of the children of Israel"* down into Babylon.

What this represents in our day is that the devil makes every effort to entice our young people out into the mean streets of our cities. He lures them outside the haven of their homes, away from their families and their church influences, and takes them into a "strange land" that they know nothing about

And even though they try their best to fit in, they still feel awkward. They feel out of place. They feel like a misfit. They put on a very good act. They play the role well. But they know they're different; that they're in an unfamiliar world.

That's exactly how the Israelis felt during the time of their captivity in Babylon. It's a dreadful feeling that is vividly described in Psalms 137:1-4.

"By the rivers of Babylon, there we sat down, yea, we wept, when we remembered Zion (Jerusalem or the city of David). We hanged our harps upon the willows in the midst thereof. For there they that wasted us, required of us mirth, saying, sing us one of the songs of Zion."

But we said *"How shall we sing the Lord's song in a strange land?"*

This reminds me of the story a pastor friend of mine related to me about a mutual friend. He was a young man whom as a child I thought resembled the late Michael Jackson when he was a child. At the time, the youngster wore his hair in an afro or natural style that was popular during the 1970's. I hung out with his older brother during my high school years. After I left home for college, I didn't have the opportunity to see my friend's younger brother grow up.

It was years later when I came into contact with this young man again. He was grown-up now and had gotten saved and was attending a church that I had attended several years before. I hardly recognized him. The huge afro hairstyle that he wore as a child was gone, replaced by a close-cropped fade haircut. He was good-looking, about five-feet-ten inches tall and slim. He had been on the high school cheer squad. And he was an excellent singer, who led songs in the local church and the district choirs.

I didn't know until later that the young man had a weakness in the area of same sex relationships prior to coming to know the Lord. And after being saved, the devil continued to tempt him, to allure him in an attempt to drag him back into the *"beggarly elements of the world"* (Galatians 4:9).

Unfortunately, the young man lost the battle and ended up sliding back into his old habits. He left the church and ended up in the streets of a large city in Ohio. My minister friend told me that one evening he was driving through a particular area of that city when he happened to see the guy. It wasn't a pretty picture. He was sitting on the curb of a street with several friends.

They were all lamenting their fate in the gutter. They were shedding tears about being in a place they really didn't want to be. They were angry at the devil for taking them there, for tricking them into believing that life could be fulfilling outside of God.

They were in a strange land, in a Babylonian nation where they didn't belong. They had sold their souls to the devil for fleeting moments of pleasure. And all the while, their minds wouldn't let them forget Zion. It wouldn't let them forget the wonderful times they spent in the presence of the Lord. The songs of praise wouldn't stop ringing in their ears.

They wanted desperately to sing them again. But they couldn't do it in the strange place they had landed. It was a place of bondage, a place that had wrapped its strong tentacles around them and refused to let them go.

Chapter 11: Do I Know You?

I remember when

I'm also a good example of how the devil lures young people out into the streets. I mentioned earlier how when I reached the age of 14, I was too old for my mother to control me any longer. I stopped attending church and "dove head-first into the sea of life".

Church turned me off. I considered it a fairy tale and a place for losers. None of my school friends went to church. They all hung out and I wanted to hit the streets too, to find out what "real life" was all about. As I related in my book, however, I found a cruel, mean world in which the devil quickly began the process of squeezing the life out of me.

What I found in the streets was a snare that had been set by the devil for the purpose of destroying me. And I ended up caught in a whirlwind that spiraled downward to an ugly place of drugs, alcohol and pretension, until the Lord rescued me.

I also had to deal with this issue as a parent. I tried very hard to make a good life for my children, to keep them away from the influence of the streets.

I was blessed to be able to move the family into suburbia. It was nice and quiet. We had access to parks and walking trails. The recreation center was within walking distance. All the neighbors worked hard to keep their yards looking good.

During the evening and night hours, you could hear the symphonic sounds of chirping insects, owls and other nocturnal creatures. Honking horns, sirens, blasting CD players in cars, and other traffic noise was virtually nonexistent. It was the perfect place to raise a family.

But my children, during their teenage years, saw it differently. In their opinion, the neighborhood was too quiet. It didn't have enough action. There were no fights on the street corners, no crowds of roving teenagers creating havoc. It was boring and dull. They wanted to move "into the city", to be where the action was.

It was a situation in which I had to be vigilant. I recognized it as the work of the devil, trying to lure my children into the wrong place where he could easily destroy them.

I did what I could to make living in the suburbs more exciting for them. I kept them involved in athletic and band activities and purchased pool and tennis tables for recreation in the home. But no matter how much I did, it wasn't enough to fend off the enemy's attack.

My children, like many young people do, would sneak off with their friends and go into the inner city to do things they shouldn't have been doing. And, I knew I had a fight on my hands.

Consequently, I had to take up arms to fight against the satanic assault. And trust me, it's not easy driving around the city late into the night, really not knowing where to look, but desperately trying to find your daughter before the crowd she's with strips her of her virtue, her dignity and her future.

It was all a part of satan's plan, to take me and then attempt to allure my children onto his turf, where he reigned, where he was king, where he was god. He wanted to take me—when I was a teenager—and then my children to a place where he could be our master, a place where when he spoke, we not only listened but would jump at his every command.

Perhaps the best example of this phenomenon is found in the Bible, in the book of Luke, chapter 15, versus 11 through 32. It's the familiar story of the "prodigal son". I'll let Jesus tell it in his words.

". . . A certain man had two sons: And the younger of them said to his father, Father, give me the portion of goods that falleth to me. And he divided unto them his living. And not many days after the younger son gathered all together, and took his journey into a far country, and there wasted his substance with riotous living.

"And when he had spent all, there arose a mighty famine in that land; and he began to be unwanted. And he went and joined himself to a citizen of that country; and he sent him into his fields to feed swine. And he would fain (gladly) have filled his belly with the husks that the swine did eat: and no man gave unto him."

When you look underneath the surface of this story, there were some distinct approaches satan used to influence the prodigal and they are the

Chapter 11: Do I Know You?

same methods he uses today with our children. Let's take a quick look at what they are and how he used them in his attempt to destroy the prodigal.

First, he enticed him to want control. *"Father, give me the portion of goods that falleth to me."* As I talked about earlier, just like satan wanted the control of heaven, one of his primary tools to influence the young is to give them a desire to control their surroundings, even when they are too immature to properly handle things.

It is a huge mistake when parents allow their children to have control, or in other words, have the ability to do whatever they want to do in spite of what the parents think. When parents do this, they effectively place their children in a position of being little "gods".

Second, satan persuaded the prodigal that he could make his own decisions, even though he obviously was too immature to do so. *"And not many days after the younger son gathered all together and took his journey. . ."*

Young people are notorious for thinking they're mature enough to make wise decisions. And while there is nothing wrong with parents allowing their children to make as many decisions as possible to help them mature, there has to be some discretion. Sometimes, you have to invoke what I call parental discretion. If a child wants to do something that's just not best for them, the parent has to step in and say "I'm sorry, you just can't do it".

The third thing the prodigal was influenced to do was *"go into a far country".* The prodigal made a terrible mistake here. He didn't just go down the block to get away, he went miles away. He left his familiar surroundings and took residence in a place he didn't know, a place where he didn't know anyone, a place that didn't reinforce the principles he'd grown up with. He didn't have the street smarts to deal with the worldliness and pace of the place and it quickly got the best of him.

Because he had a lot of money, he was initially befriended by a lot of people whose motives weren't pure. The prodigal thought he was popular and liked. He thought he was a big shot. But he soon found out he wasn't what he thought. His so-called friends quickly exploited him and took everything he had. As soon as his money dried up, they abandoned him to find someone else they could take advantage of.

I don't have a problem with children growing up, getting out of high school and going away from home to college, the military or some other area of life. Children have to be able to take on personal responsibility and accountability at some point in life. And, we as parents, have to be willing to "release" them like the proverbial mother eagle when it's teaching its young to fly.

The eagle first hovers over the nest to demonstrate how wings are used. Later, it uses its beak to push the little eaglets over the side of the nest, forcing them to flap their wings so they can learn how to fly.

Now, the mother eagle doesn't let her babies fall to their deaths. If they don't start flapping their wings and flying, the mother swoops down and catches them. But after returning them to the nest, she pushes them out again. She continues doing so, until the babies begin to flap their wings in the necessary rhythmic pattern that lifts them off in flight. At that point, the baby is on its own.

The prodigal, just like most young people who think they're more mature than they really are, clearly wasn't ready to be on his own. He hadn't yet learned to fly. And the last mistake he made was *"joining himself to a citizen of that country"*.

Too often when young people leave home and find themselves in trouble, rather than calling a family member or a long-time family friend, they hook up with someone in their new environment, someone they have no history with and doesn't genuinely care for their welfare.

The prodigal connected himself with a person who saw him as free labor. That person quickly put him to work in the fields feeding the swine (hogs). He didn't clean him up. He didn't dress him up. He didn't give him a warm bath or a hot plate of food. And there the young man stood, a tragic, defeated shell of what he used to be.

The story of the prodigal son is a powerful story of a young man whom allows himself to be enticed away from his loving family and home where he had access to everything he needed to live. He was beguiled into thinking that he "was a man now" and it was time for him to go out and experience life.

What the young man found was an unfamiliar world where people only like you or gravitate to you when you've got something to offer them. He discovered a world where friends are fickle and forsake you in a skinny minute when your money runs out.

The "prodigal" ended up in the swine fields, thinking about eating the husks the swine were eating.

He was like far too many of our young people today who let the enticement of the devil steal them away from what is familiar and most distressingly away from their families and the God who dearly loves them.

Fortunately, for the prodigal, the dreadful condition he was in caused him to "come to himself". He remembered what he had back home, a loving father and family, all the conveniences anyone could want. He turned his heart and mind back toward home, pulled himself up out of the slop and went back to the loving environment he almost lost forever.

If only all our children can come to themselves in this manner before tragedy occurs.

Nebuchadnezzar Is After My Child

Chapter 12

You Are What You Eat

*" Now the serpent was more subtil than any beast of the field. . .
And he said unto the woman, Yea, hath God said,
Ye shall not eat of every tree of the garden?"*

~ Genesis 3: 1

The next strategy Nebuchadnezzar used against the Hebrew children was to change their eating habits. These young men were well schooled in the Levitical laws governing what the Israelis were to eat.

But, you'll see in verse five of Daniel, chapter 1, Nebuchadnezzar ordered that the Israeli youth be *"appointed daily provision of the king's meat and of the wine which he drank"*.

The king's intention was to completely change the diet of the young Israelis from spiritual to worldly. He wanted to totally contradict what they had formally been taught regarding what they were to eat, which would have gone completely against their principles and the commandments of their God.

The food King Nebuchadnezzar wanted them to eat and the wine he wanted them to drink was the same food and wine the Babylonians offered to idols. To eat such food would have been disobeying God's laws; to drink such wine would have dulled their minds because of its intoxicating effects.

There's an adage that says "you are what you eat". The phrase typically refers to the types of food a person eats and its impact on their health. It is also used to mean whatever a person is exposed to or whatever a person takes into their system (their mind, their heart) that's what they ultimately become.

An example is the infant who is born in France to French-speaking parents. If you take that baby out of France and away from its French-speaking parents before it has learned to speak, bring it to America to live with English-speaking parents, that child will ultimately speak English.

Yes, it was born French and would have learned the French language had it remained in France with its birth parents. But by simply changing the "diet" of what the baby took in, you make it into something different than what it was born to be.

This is a simple example, but it aligns with how the devil deceived Eve in the Garden of Eden. He enticed her to eat the only food God had forbidden her and Adam to eat—and it immediately turned her into a different person.

No longer was she chaste and pure of sin. She was changed into a sinner who'd disobeyed God and suffered the consequences of being cast out of paradise. She was no longer the woman God had created her to be.

That's exactly the type of strategy the devil has used for centuries and is continuing to use against young people today. He entices them away from the country or environment of their birth and takes them to a country of a different language, a country of a different mindset, a country where there are no morals and values.

One of the first changes that occurs when a child is lured outside of their home environment is the way they talk. They pick up the slang, the street jargon, the cool talk. Words like "hatin" (putting someone down), "yolo" (you only live once), "turnt" (drunk), "shade or thrownin' shade" (subtly talking bad about someone), "on fleek" (cool or tight), "bye Felicia" (say goodbye in a sassy manner) and "Bae" (before anyone else) become a regular part of their vocabulary.

They also start acting different. They start walking different. They develop a limp in their stride.

There are many "worldly" influences that come into play that make youth become different. There's the automatic influence of their peers and their desire to fit in. But perhaps one of the most prominent today is the influence of media—television, video, music, etc.

There have been many studies conducted and a tremendous amount of debate surrounding the impact of media on our youth today. The studies and debates have involved a host of perspectives ranging from those of

Chapter 12: You Are What You Eat

secular scholars, to politicians, sociologists and psychologists to Christians.

The prevailing opinion among many psychologists and most Christians is that modern media do in fact have a great degree of influence on the way young people think and behave. I personally contend it has an immense influence, particularly as it relates to how young people view authority, sexuality, relationships, drug and alcohol use and perhaps most disturbingly violence.

Take for example the conclusions drawn in 1999 by some of the youth who attended Columbine High School in Littleton, Colo., after Dylan Klebold and Eric Harris killed 15 people, including themselves, and injured 21 others.

In a USA Today newspaper article, Columbine students Christine Pope and Chad Douglas described their belief that the Columbine killers, Klebold and Harris, were influenced by the music they listened to and the computer games they played. The article pointed out that the two had a hangout where they would listen to music with explicit lyrics and play violent video games filled with blood and gore.

Pope, a sophomore at Columbine at the time, said, "I think that the music we listen to and the television we watch influences us in the way we dress, the things we say and the way we act. It definitely influences society as a whole".

Douglas, also a sophomore said, "Music and television has an effect on the way we act. If you listen to church music and then rap music, you will have two totally different perspectives."

The lead paragraph in the article, written by Anna Kirby, said "From South Park to Friends and Marilyn Manson to No Limit Soldiers, the music and television teens listen to today is inundated with profanity, sexual references and drugs."

And, there's much, much more.

Chapter 13

The devil IS Making Them do it!

"And the serpent said unto the woman, ye shall not surely die:"

~ Genesis 3:4

If you're a baby boomer, I'm sure you remember the television comedian Flip Wilson. Flip hosted a weekly variety TV series in which he popularized the saying "the devil made me do it".

After Flip's slogan was popularized, many people started blaming the devil for their misbehavior. Initially, much of it was done in jest, but over time it became the excuse of choice.

The problem is, in actuality while people have used the slogan as an easy excuse to do wrong and justify their wrongdoing, the devil IS behind it. He IS making them do it, largely through the direct influence of the television, movie, music and video game entertainment industries. That's why it's no coincidence that the classmates of Klebold and Harris pointed to the influence media had on them.

Many of us can remember when television and music on our radios were tame and family-friendly. However, the advent of unregulated cable television back in the 1980's, with its explicit music videos shown on such stations as MTV (Music Television), HBO (Home Box Office) and Showtime helped launch a trend of risqué (sexually suggestive) and violence-oriented programming throughout media.

And, now with a multitude of cable outlets and the explosion of digital media, R and X-rated programming is common—and within easy reach of young people like Klebod and Harris. Both of them spent countless hours to become experts at a video-game called Doom. This game was popular in the 1990's and known as an early example of the first-person shooter genre. According to reports, while the boys were preparing their attack, Harris said the killing would be like playing Doom.

Yes, I know there are many experts who contend there is no causal relationship between young people watching violent television programming, listening to violence-laced music or playing violent video games and them committing violent acts or behaving violently.

And, I know that the manufacturers of these games argue the same thing. After all, there are billions of dollars being made off these products.

But other reputable experts strongly disagree. Their extensive research and sound facts tell a completely different story. They make it very clear that our young people are being influenced to commit violence as a result of being bombarded with violence-packed new-age media, with video games being the leader of the pack.

There has been continuing research about the issue of how media—particularly violence-oriented programming—affects young people since television began. For example, based on 15 years of "consistently disturbing" findings about the violent content of children's programs, the Surgeon General's Scientific Advisory Committee on Television and Social Behavior was formed in 1969 to assess the impact of violence on the attitudes, values and behavior of viewers. The resulting report and a follow-up report in 1982 by the National Institute of Mental Health identified these major effects of seeing violence on television:

- Children may become less sensitive to the pain and suffering of others.
- Children may be more fearful of the world around them.
- Children may be more likely to behave in aggressive or harmful ways toward others.

Research by Psychologists L. Rowell Huesmann, Leonard Eron and others starting in the 1980s found that children who watched many hours of violence on television when they were in elementary school tended to show higher levels of aggressive behavior when they became teenagers.

By observing these participants into adulthood, Huesmann and Eron found that the ones who'd watched a lot of TV violence when they were eight years old were more likely to be arrested and prosecuted for criminal acts as adults.

In fact Dr. Eron, who is deceased, accumulated over 50 years of research about the impact of media violence on youth. In 1992, at the time

Chapter 13: The devil IS Making Them do it!

chair of the American Psychological Association Commission on Youth and Violence, he testified before the U.S. Senate Committee on Governmental Affairs that:

"There can no longer be any doubt that heavy exposure to televised violence is one of the causes of aggressive behavior, crime and violence in society. The evidence comes from both the laboratory and real-life studies." He went on to say that the effect of televised violence can be seen in children of all ages, in girls as well as boys, and in children of all levels of intelligence and socioeconomic status.

This area of research has picked up significant steam in recent years due to the increasing variety of media that is exposing young people to massively escalating levels of violence. Along with that is the widespread concern about the magnitude of violence being committed by our young, particularly as it relates to the shocking massacre at Columbine High School.

Soon after the Columbine slaughter, in July 26, 2000, six highly-reputable, national health associations issued a Joint Statement on the Impact of Entertainment Violence on Children, definitively linking violence in television, music, video games and movies to increased aggression in children.

Those agencies included the American Health Association, American Academy of Pediatrics, American Psychological Association, American Psychiatric Association, American Academy of Family Physicians and the American Academy of Child & Adolescent Psychiatry.

The statement was the centerpiece of a public health summit on entertainment violence organized by Sam Brownback, whom at the time was a Republican Senator from Kansas and as of this writing is Governor of that state. Two panels of experts, one of which discussed traditional media, such as television and movies, and another which focused on the newer field of interactive technologies, such as video games, convened at the conference.

Their Statement said: "Viewing entertainment violence can lead to increase in aggressive attitudes, values and behavior, particularly in children. Its effects are measurable and long lasting. Moreover, prolonged viewing of media violence can lead to emotional desensitization toward violence in real life.

The Statement said well over 1,000 studies had been conducted which pointed overwhelmingly to a causal connection between teen violence and viewing entertainment violence.

Advocating a code of conduct for the entire entertainment industry, Brownback compared the initiative by the medical community to a declaration that cigarettes can cause cancer.

Statement Called A Turning Point

"I think this is an important turning point," said Brownback. "Among the professional community, there's no longer any doubt about this. For the first time, you have the four major medical and psychiatric associations coming together and stating flatly that violence in entertainment has a direct effect on violence in our children."

Since the Joint Statement came out in the year 2000, many other respected organizations have chimed in about the effects of media violence on youth.

The U.S. Secret Service and the U.S. Department of Education issued a report in 2002 based on the examination of 37 incidents of targeted school shootings and school attacks from 1974 to 2000 in this country. The report found that "over half of the attackers demonstrated some interest in violence through movies, video games, books, and other media."

According to data from the Pew Research Center, many of the most popular video games, such as "Call of Duty" and "Grand Theft Auto," are extremely violent; and several meta-analytic reviews have reported negative effects on youth due to exposure to violence in video games.

Pew reported that a 2010 review by psychologist Craig A. Anderson and others concluded that "the evidence strongly suggests that exposure to violent video games is a causal risk factor for increased aggressive behavior, aggressive cognition, and aggressive affect and for decreased empathy and prosocial behavior."

An October 5, 2012 article in Psychiatric Times, the Media Violence Commission of the International Society for Research on Aggression

Chapter 13: The devil IS Making Them do it!

(ISRA) said in a report on media violence, "Over the past 50 years, a large number of studies conducted around the world have shown that watching violent television, watching violent films, or playing violent video games increases the likelihood for aggressive behavior."

If that's not enough, a November 2013 report by the American Psychological Association said the Pew Research Center found that 97 percent of adolescents age 12-17 play video games—on a computer, on consoles such as the Wii, Playstation and Xbox, or on portable devices such as Gameboys, smartphones and tablets.

Despite these studies and alarms that have been sounded about the impact of media violence, the intensity of the violence in media has exponentially increased due to its vast popularity. And, many of the most violent video games are even promoted in media commercials by prominent professional athletes.

The disturbing result of the widespread promotion of these games is that the carnage has continued.

Since Columbine, there have been a glut of other seemingly senseless mass shootings, including those by young people at Virginia Tech University in 2007 where 32 people were killed; Sandy Hook Elementary School in Newtown, Ct., in 2012 where 26 people—mostly small children —were killed; the Aurora, Colo., theater in 2012 where six were killed and 13 injured; and the Mother Emmanuel Church in Charleston, SC, in 2015 where nine people attending a Bible study were gunned down.

In nearly every case, investigators found that the young killers were obsessed with violent-oriented music or video games such as Combat Arms, Counterstrike, Grand Theft Auto and Call of Duty.

One of the most powerful arguments that violence in media influences young people to kill has been made by Lt. Col. Dave Grossman. Grossman, retired from the U.S Army but now is a psychology and military science professor at West Point, in 1999 published the book "On Killing: The Psychological Cost of Learning to Kill in War and Society". The book examines the army's conditioning techniques used to overcome soldiers' aversion to killing.

After meeting Gloria DeGaetano, a media literacy educator and CEO of Parent Coach International, who had been helping parents and professionals understand the conditioning effects of violent media from the perspective of a child and adolescent brain vulnerabilities, Grossman corroborated with her to publish a revised and updated version of Killing in 2014.

They aptly renamed the book "Stop Teaching Our Kids To Kill". They concluded that the same methods used by the military to teach soldiers to kill without feeling were being used by media to teach young people to kill in the same manner.

Grossman states in the book's introduction: "We wanted parents, educators, law enforcement officers . . . to know without equivocation that media violence harms. We wanted to make people aware of how the prolific use of sensational violence in television, movies and in video games affects kids' attitudes and actions."

Grossman said later in the book that "Violent movies are targeted at the young, both men and women, the same audience the military has determined to be most susceptible for its killing purposes. Violent video games hardwire young people for shooting at humans. The entertainment industry conditions the young in exactly the same way the military does. Civilian society apes the training and conditioning techniques of the military at its peril."

Grossman and DeGaetano noted that while violent video games play a prominent role, they aren't the only media culprit that's influencing youth to kill. Television and movies are also at fault. They report that according to statistics, children in the U.S. between the ages of eight and 18 spend on average 40 hours a week with screen technologies, not counting the time they spend on iPads, laptops and computers at school.

During those 40 hours, they see and experience extraordinary amounts of gruesome content since 90 percent of movies and 60 percent of TV shows depict graphic violent imagery. In fact, they say, by age 18 a U.S. youth will have seen at least 40,000 simulated murders and 200,000 acts of violence on television alone.

And, this massive viewing of violence isn't relegated just to causing kids to kill. It's creating immense violence-related havoc in a number of

Chapter 13: The devil IS Making Them do it!

other ways throughout our society, as well. Look at these statistics from the Center for Disease Control (CDC), for the year 2010.
- 4,828 young people, ages 10-24, were victims of homicide; an average of 13 each day.
- 82.8% of of youth homicides were committed with a firearm.
- Juveniles under 18 accounted for 13.7 percent of all violent crime arrests and 22.5 percent of all property crime arrests.
- 784 juveniles were arrested for murder.
- 2,198 juveniles were arrested for forcible rape.
- 35,001 juveniles were arrested for aggravated assault.

This is a crisis of epic proportions that our society has not been able to get a handle on. The streets, schools and parks of our country have become battle grounds where violence has become a way of life for far too many of our kids.

Gone are the days when it was safe for kids to walk to school and enjoy learning without fear.

The sad result is that the lives of our youth are being stolen away. They're being destroyed through death, imprisonment, injury or fear.

Do you remember when?

"Try to remember the times in September when life was young and oh so mellow. Try to remember, it's nice to remember and follow."

Do you remember that song? I became familiar with it my last year in high school. While visiting a good friend, an album titled "In A Mellow Mood" by the renowned Motown group Temptations was playing. The album was a collection of classic stage play songs, including "Try to Remember" from the musical comedy *The Fantasticks*.

My friend, and it seemed all his sisters, had excellent singing voices. I loved going to their home because it was always filled with what my mother called the "blues", which we couldn't listen to in our house. All I knew was that I loved listening to the mellow sounds of the Motown singers that emanated from the 45 singles and 33 albums my friend's family always played.

I immediately fell in love with the words and melody of *"Try to Remember"* and years later was able to enjoy the stage play version.

"Try to remember the times in September when life was young and oh so mellow." The words come to my mind often. The older I've gotten, the more they seem to come.

The words make me think about how innocent our world used to be, even during the years I was growing up in the turbulent sixties and seventies. Children could walk to school without concern of being abducted. Even at night, we walked all over town to sporting events, community center dances and house parties.

Our parents had no concern about something happening to us as we roamed the streets, visiting our friends, boyfriends or girlfriends, and seeking out the next party or dance.

It was mellow, as the song lyrics say. It was peaceful and calm.

Another song that often comes to mind about the "good old days" was produced by the Gospel group, the Winans. It was on an album the group released entitled *Tomorrow and More*. The song - *Bring Back the Days of Yea and Nay* - has a similar message as *Try to Remember*. Here are some of the words:

"I remember when life was so simple
You did or you didn't
You would or you wouldn't
But it ain't like that anymore

I remember when life was so easy
People said what they meant
They were either for it or against it
But it ain't like that anymore
Somewhere, we lost the score"

Bring back the time when we could see
What it was we were to be
Caught in the midst of complexities
We search for yea and nay

Chapter 13: The devil IS Making Them do it!

We knew where we belonged
What was right and what was wrong

    The Winans were absolutely right - it ain't like that anymore. Worse yet, their song was released in 1984. It was bad then, but those times can't compare with how bad it is now.

    Where have the good old days gone?

    They've gone the way of cable and internet television and radio and it's influx of risqué, no limits programming.

    They've gone the way of violence-laced video games that young people spend countless hours playing and infusing their minds and hearts with thoughts of killing and being killed.

    They've gone the way of the devil using these modern-day entertainment instruments to influence our youth to self-destruct.

Nebuchadnezzar Is After My Child

Part III

The Thief Cometh To Destroy!

Chapter 14

Satan's Tentacles Have Stretched Into The New Millennium

"Be sober, be vigilant; because your adversary the devil, as a roaring lion, walketh about, seeking whom he may devour;"

~ 1 Peter 5:8

Just like King Nebuchadnezzar brazenly stole the best youth of Judah, Satan as a roaring lion is walking about today seeking young people he can devour (I Peter 5:8).

And he has clearly used cable and internet television, music and video gaming, with their heavy emphasis on violence, to take a substantial toll on our youth. But the creation and immense popularity of social media has added a whole new, complicated and dangerous dimension.

Television is fast becoming old hat with today's young people. They are a mobile generation that's gotten increasingly too restless to sit down and watch conventional TV programming. They get their entertainment via mobile devices like cell phones, tablets or computers. And, the majority of that entertainment involves participation on social media sites.

It's a trend that's grown so rapidly, big and small companies have been forced to change the way they market their products to the young. They have to do it in a fashion that's fit for the small screens young people carry in their pockets or backpacks.

So how did this social media revolution come to be and how exactly is satan capitalizing on its massive popularity?

It started in the 1960's. That's when, according to an article posted May 8, 2013 by online publication *Small Business Trends*, the first type of social media began with the emergence of electronic mail or email communication.

But email has limitations when it comes to creating communities of people who want to interact socially. And, as it is in our fast-paced, ultra-modern world, some smart people capitalized on that limitation, consequently inventing social media technologies that have taken the world by storm.

According to *Small Business Trends*, the first recognizable modern-day social media site, Six Degrees, was created in 1997. It enabled users to upload profiles and make friends with other users. In 1999, blogging sites became popular, and their popularity helped propel to prominence more comprehensive social media sites like MySpace and LinkedIn in the early 2000s. And, sites like Photobucket and Flickr facilitated online photo sharing.

YouTube came out in 2005, creating a way for people to communicate and share with each other by way of video across great distances. By 2006, Facebook and Twitter both became available to users throughout the world.

Today, social media is the dominant form of communication used by young people. In fact, for the past decade, with more than 1.2 billion daily active users as of December 2016, Facebook has been the prominent social media used by people worldwide.

This kind of mass usage is a clear indication that social media is a phenomenon that's not going away. And, just like satan always does, he takes things that are meant to be positive and turns them into instruments he can use for his own wicked motives. And, that's exactly what he's done with social media, causing it to become one of the most destructive devices he's now using to destroy our youth.

Here's a sampling of what I mean:

The Huffington Post ran a blog on May 25, 2015 that addressed what it called an alarming trend related to social media use among young people. The blog, titled *Influence of Social Media on Teenagers* reported that "According to a report by Common Sense Media, 75 percent of teenagers in America currently have profiles on social networking sites, of which 68 percent use Facebook as their main social networking tool".

The blog noted that "While social networking undoubtedly plays a vital role in broadening social connections and learning technical skills, its risks

Chapter 14: Satan's Tentacles Have Stretched Into The New Millennium

cannot be overlooked. The lack or difficulty in self-regulation and susceptibility to peer pressure makes adolescents vulnerable to such evils as Facebook depression, sexting and cyberbullying, which are realistic threats.

Cyberbullying ranges from direct threatening and unpleasant emails to anonymous activities such as trolling. Trolling, the act of deliberately inflicting hatred, bigotry, racism, misogyny, or just simple bickering between people, often anonymously, is also pervasive in social networking. If you thought trolls lived under a bridge, 28 percent of America lives there, it seems."

If cyberbullying isn't bad enough, Common Sense Media, posted an article on March 1, 2016 noting that increasing numbers of young people have gotten bored with Facebook and have moved on to social media applications (apps) that give them more freedom and secrecy from their parents and other authority figures.

The article described 16 such apps which let teens do it all - text, chat, meet people, and share their photos and videos. The list of apps described included Kik Messenger, WhatsApp, Tumblr, Periscope, GroupMe, Snapchat, Whisper. And, the potential dangers posed to youth by some of them is very troubling to say the least. For example:

- **Stranger danger is an issue** with Kik Messenger. It allows communication with strangers who share their Kik usernames to find people to chat with. The app allegedly has been used in high profile crimes, including the murder of a 13-year-old girl[9] and a child-pornography[10] case.
- **Porn is easy to find on Tumblr.** This online hangout is hip and creative but sometimes raunchy. Pornographic images and videos and depictions of violence, self-harm, drug use, and offensive language are easily searchable.
- **Whispers are often sexual in nature.** Some users use the app to try to hook up with people nearby, while others post "confessions" of desire. Lots of eye-catching, nearly nude pics accompany these shared secrets.

The article also cautioned parents about sexting, the action of sending sexually revealing pictures of themselves or sexually explicit messages to another individual or group. It said sexting is now a common activity among the teen community using these social media.

Perhaps more alarming is an internet report posted in July, 2015 by WCNC.com, the online publication of the CBS television affiliate in Raleigh, NC.

The report said the FBI is warning parents about a crime that's growing as fast as social media. It's called Sextortion. Predators meet people online, coerce them into sending sexually explicit pictures or videos, and then use those images as blackmail.

The FBI defines it as a criminal act that occurs when someone demands something of value, typically images of a sexual nature, sexual favors, or money, from a person by either:

- Threatening to release or distribute material the victim seeks to keep private, such as sexually explicit images, videos, e-mail, and text messages.
- Threatening to financially harm friends or relatives of the victim by using information obtained from the victim's computer unless they comply with demands.

The WCNC.com report said according to the National Center for Missing and Exploited Children, 76 percent of incidents involve female children and 11 percent involve male children. The organization said the average age at the time of the incident was approximately 15 years old.

It's a nightmare for parents that's happening all over the country. And, it's not going away.

TurboFuture.com, an internet site run by computer and technology experts, posted an article October 12, 2015 that said teenagers spend an average of 27 hours online per week. That's over half the time of a work week.

Chapter 14: Satan's Tentacles Have Stretched Into The New Millennium

The article fairly said that while social media have become prominent parts of life for many young people, most don't stop to think about what the effects are on their lives, whether positive or negative.

"Are we as a society becoming more concerned with Facebook 'friends' than we are with the people we interact with face-to-face in our daily lives?" the article asked. "What will the longterm effects . . . be?"

For starters, the article noted that already:

- Extensive online engagement is correlated with personality and brain disorders like poor social skills, ADHD, narcissistic tendencies, a need for instant gratification, and addictive behaviors and other emotional distress like depression, anxiety, and loneliness.
- Children at higher risk for depression, low self-esteem, and eating disorders are more prone to feeling isolated and disconnected (especially youth with disabilities).

And, then there's the "FoMO" or fear of missing out phenomenon. Here's the definition provided by Wikipedia.

"**FoMO** is "a pervasive apprehension that others might be having rewarding experiences from which one is absent". This social angst is characterized by "a desire to stay continually connected with what others are doing". FoMO is also defined as a fear of regret, which may lead to a compulsive concern that one might miss an opportunity for social interaction, a novel experience, profitable investment or other satisfying events. In other words, FoMO perpetuates the fear of having made the wrong decision on how to spend time, as "you can imagine how things could be different".

Don't trust Wikipedia? Believe it or not the word FoMO has even been added to the Oxford English Dictionary. It's hard to believe, but it's true. Here's the definition given by the Oxford English Dictionary: "Anxiety that an exciting or interesting event may currently be happening elsewhere, often aroused by posts seen on a social media website".

As you can see, the devil has latched onto social media and is using it like a vicious drug to addict and destroy the lives of young people. And, his ruthlessness knows no bounds, as attested by the following news reports about incidents that are so bizarre, they're very hard to believe they actually happened. But they did.

- Scott Humphrey, 27 at the time, was sentenced to over four years in jail after repeatedly punching his friend for "poking" his girlfriend on Facebook. The friend, who was bleeding profusely from the punches, fell, hit his head and died. *(The dailymail.com, 10/5/2014)*

- Fifteen-year-old Hughstan Schlicker was addicted to MySpace. He'd been threatening on the site to kill himself for several weeks. His dad was concerned and banned him from using the site. Being cut off from the digital world, Schlicker said he "felt like I was stabbed with a knife and it went straight through and no matter how hard I pulled, I couldn't pull out the knife. . ." He subsequently called in sick from school with the intent to kill himself—unless his dad arrived home from work before 4 p.m. Sadly, that day his dad got home before 4 and his son followed him into their kitchen and shot him with a 12-gauge shotgun. *(Fox News, 3/6/2008)*

- Torrie Lynn Emery, 23, and Danielle Booth, 20, were having a Facebook feud for months over a guy who'd been in jail over a year. One day Torrie saw Danielle riding in a car driven by a friend. Torrie, with her three-year-old daughter in the backseat, still decided to pursue Danielle. A high-speed car chase ensued, with Torrie ramming the other car several times, ultimately causing the driver to run a red light and hit a dump truck. The driver died instantly and Danielle was critically injured. Torrie was found guilty of second degree murder and was facing an 18-60 year sentence at the time of this writing. *(CBS News, 9/24/2010)*

- Amidst a digital sea of teen girls listing their hobbies as 'shopping,' or 'Katy Perry,' 15 year-old Alyssa Bustamante stood out like a special

Chapter 14: Satan's Tentacles Have Stretched Into The New Millennium

snowflake. Her Facebook profile interests included 'cutting' and 'killing people.' And she wasn't lying... After planning the crime for months—going so far as to dig a shallow grave in advance—Alyssa stabbed her nine-year-old neighbor to death. She was permanently instated in a mental institution. *(CBS News - 11/25/2009)*

- Childhood friends Jameg Blake and Kwame Dancy had been exchanging heated 140-character insults on Twitter for days over a woman both men liked. The feud escalated to the point threats were made. A confrontation ensued in the luxury NYC high-rise where the 22-year-olds lived on the same floor. Kwame taunted Blake and told him to "chill". Blake did not chill. Instead, he retrieved a shotgun and shot Kwame in the neck, killing him. Immediately after, he tweeted, "R.I.P. Kwame." Blake was sentenced to 21 years in prison for manslaughter. *(Mashable, 1/10/2010)*

- A few weeks away from graduation, a young man in Indiana was killed as the result of a feud on Twitter. The tension started when Jerrold Parker, 18, tweeted at his soon-to-be killer Devin Leggett that Leggett "couldn't rap." They got into a back and forth argument about who could rap best. Not too long later, Leggett, 19, shot Parker multiple times, according to multiple witnesses. Leggett was charged with murder and carrying a handgun without a license. *(Indianapolis Star, 3/1/2016)*

As mentioned, these stories are unbelievable, but true. Who would have thought social media—designed to stimulate conversations and connect people with friends and family—would turn out to be such a powerful tool for destruction.

The devil has seized the opportunity to use this tool to his advantage in his relentless pursuit of destroying our young. He's using social media to influence people to create false images of themselves in an attempt to impress. He's using it to pump up egos and disguise low self-esteem. He's using it to lure young people into dangerous places of bullying and sexual assault. And, sadly, he's using it to kill.

Chapter 15

But I Don't Like My Name

"I told Jesus it would be alright if he changed my name."

~ Christian hymn also sung by Nina Simone and Roberta Flack

It's frightening when you think about the depth of influence satan and subsequently our new-age society has over how we think about life, living and about ourselves. I connect satan and society because the Bible explains that *"satan is the prince and power of the air" (Ephesians 2:2)*, meaning he's the one behind the "worldly system" that exists. He's the one largely responsible for influencing how people in our society think and behave.

That's why as soon as we're old enough to have some sense or consciousness about being accepted by others, we start trying to remake ourselves. We start trying to change who we are. We start trying to change our identity into something that's cool and hip and that conforms to the mainstream of the world around us.

I started taking myself through this metamorphosis, just like everyone around me, at a very early age. The way this process started in me was characteristic of the times. It was during the early 1960's when our American society was starting to separate at the seams politically, racially and religiously.

I became very shy and self-conscious about how I looked mainly due to a racial incident that happened to me during my fifth grade school year.

My teacher's name was Mr. Reddick. Mr. Reddick is the only teacher I had during elementary school whose name I still remember, for obvious reasons. His influence left a lasting impression on my psyche.

Mr. Reddick was a middle-age, white man who was prone to say things that were inappropriate in the presence of 10 and 11-year-old kids. He also was the first person I knew that I'd call a real racist.

I say this because Mr. Reddick said something to me that I've carried with me throughout my life. One day while strutting around the room in one of his joke-telling moods, he stopped in front of my desk. He leaned down and looked at me with a smirky smile on his face, then blurted for all the class to hear:

"Boy you've got some big lips on you. Where did you get them things from?" Then he laughed and walked away.

I didn't know what the word belittled meant at the time, but that's exactly how I felt. I felt low. I felt embarrassed. I kept my head down because I felt like everybody in the class was staring at me. It was also right then and there that I started pursing my lips together, tucking them inside my mouth to hide them from view.

And I've been using this technique in an attempt to hide them ever since. I'm much more comfortable with who I am and how I look today, but tucking my lips became a habit that's been very hard for me to break.

Changing who I am

Since my self-esteem was so low already, it was easy for it to be further bruised when the guys in my sixth grade class made fun of me every time I answered when our teacher called for Terri, or Terri answered when the teacher called for me. That's right, Terri. We had a girl in the class whose name was Terri, spelled with an "i" at the end. Terri wasn't what we guys in the class considered very attractive compared to the other girls. Most of the guys joked about how she looked.

Being identified with Terri during grade school definitely wasn't something I wanted. Initially, I didn't know what to do about it. Finally, the answer came. It was during a time my mother's sister, Aunt Doll, was visiting from Alabama. I'd been thinking long and hard about how to handle this embarrassing situation when it dawned on me while walking home from school one day. I decided to bounce the idea off Aunt Doll.

"Why that's a great idea," Aunt Doll responded after I told her my plan. "Using a shortened version of your name will probably solve the problem," she said. "Now the question is what is the shorter version of Terry?"

After throwing out a bunch of names that didn't seem to work, it finally came to us. It was Ted. That's what I'd become. The next day I asked the

Chapter 15: But I Don't Like My Name

teacher to call me Ted from then on and to advise the class that I should be referred to as Ted. This would eliminate all confusion about whom she was calling on when she used the name Terri.

The plan worked like a charm, so well in fact, that even today when I run into people I graduated from high school with or people I hung out in the streets with, some still refer to me as Ted. Even several of my brothers continue to call me Ted.

Everybody thought that was cool enough, so it wasn't necessary for the guys in the streets to call me something related to my street exploits, something related to how I looked or something related to how I lived, which are the typical ways most people get their street names.

But it wasn't long before the influence of the streets started being reflected in my new name. During my later teenage years, after I had gotten a lot more "cool" or "hip", I started telling everybody the letters TED stood for "The Everlasting Dream".

Of course, the coolest way to get a name attached to you was based on outstanding street exploits. One example of this type of name is Hammer, attached to a person who had hammered somebody real good during a fight. Another example is "Slick" for someone who was better than most at conning or tricking people out of money or some other valuable commodity.

The other way you got a "name" was based on an unusually distinguishing feature a person might have, such as a big head, a big forehead or the size of their stature. Examples of names some of the people in my home town got as a result of these types of physical characteristics included Head, Big Fo (forehead) and Bugs.

But there were many other reasons people got names. And my hometown of Lima was flooded with an array of strange and unusual ones. There were names like Soup, Jigaboo, Monk, Curly, Peachy, Bubble, Bud, Lurch, Piggy, Bay Roach, Sap, Teeny, Red and Blue.

The coolest combination of names I've ever been associated with was on my college campus. Red and Blue, my homeboys, attended the same college I did. While there, they hooked up with a guy "named" White. Hence, the trio was referred to as Red, White and Blue.

Many years ago, this idea of taking on street names to change how you were identified was confined mainly to urban city areas. Back then, there were places in the country where parents could move to shield their children from the influences of street mentality, drugs and gangs.

But Satan has stretched his tentacles into every nook and cranny of our society now, from the concrete corners of inner cities to the lush, landscaped scenery of suburbia to the slow, laid-back sultry south.

Who would have thought that a quaint, southern town like Aiken, SC, where successful professionals go to enjoy their retirement years in homes that help landscape golf courses, would be battling the influx of gangs and drugs - and kids with names from the street. But it's there.

A few years ago, I read with interest an article in the *Aiken Standard* newspaper about the growing problem of gangs in Aiken. The article made particular note of the kinds of names the gang members were going by. It listed names like Shy-Boy, Joker, Frosty, Oldy, Casper and Flaco.

They were cool names, intended to identify with the gang members' personalities, or perhaps even more dangerously, their street exploits.

Chapter 16

Mpingo Jua, Hananiah, Mishael, Azariah and Daniel

*"This name you've given me is mine to keep.
It sings to me in wakefulness or sleep."*

~ from the poem The Name You've Given Me, by Eileen Manassian

The 60's and early 70's were the heyday of the Black awareness period. It was a time when African Americans were fighting for civil rights and starting to take great pride in their African Ancestry, as well as in the African nations they had come from. They were finding out they had come from royalty as opposed to the jungle natives media often portrayed them being related to at that time.

In order to better relate to their royal heritage, it became popular for African Americans to reject the Americanized names they had been given by their slave-owners and legally change their names to something representative of their homeland. In some cases, someone who was close to you dubbed you with a name.

I was given a name by my high school girlfriend when we were in college during the early 70's. My girlfriend was highly intelligent and much more learned than I was at the time, so when she initially dubbed me with the Swahili name Mpingo Jua, I had no idea what it meant. If she told me the meaning of it, I was so caught up in how cool the name sounded, I didn't hear it, or quickly forgot it.

As far as I was concerned, giving me that name was a sign of the social consciousness she had related to the African-American civil rights movement. Since I was devoted to the movement, I also believed her giving me the name was a sign of the true love and respect she had for me at the time.

It was many years later when I decided to research the name to understand it's meaning. I was astounded at what I learned.

Mpingo Jua means Ebony Sun and can be further translated Black Star. The significance of the name wasn't apparent to me at the time, but it obviously was to my girlfriend. She, like my 9th grade english teacher, saw something in me that I didn't see.

I like to believe that she saw me becoming a Black Star, an African-American whose life would ultimately shine; a life that would become a beacon of light for others to see, a ray of hope for people who come from humble beginnings.

I honestly believe what she saw came true since I became the first child in my family to obtain a college degree, the first to work in corporate America and have a stellar career with three Fortune 100 companies and most importantly become a minister of the gospel.

As a result of my professional and ministerial careers, I've been blessed to work with many schools, social service organizations and churches, give hundreds of motivational speeches, seminars and workshops and minister through preaching and teaching to thousands of people.

So yes, I believe God blessed me to become a Black Star.

Consequently, I've referred to the name Mpingo Jua a lot over the years. It has been a reminder of just how far God has brought me. And, now when I look at the meaning of names in context with the names people were given in the Bible days, it has even greater significance to me.

In Biblical days, and still today in some segments of the world, names that were and are given to newborns have specific or particular meaning. They have a significance that represents the person's character, potential or bloodline.

One of the greatest Biblical examples of this is the name Moses, which means "drawn from the water". The ultimate example is Jesus, which means "Jehovah saves". Remember the scripture in Matthew chapter one, verse 21, which says *"and she shall bring forth a son, and thou shalt call his name Jesus, for he shall save his people from their sins"*.

Since I was saved when my children were born, I felt it was important for me to give them names that had meaning. Consequently, a lot of thought went into the names they were given.

Chapter 16: Mpingo Jua, Hananiah, Mishael, Azariah, and Daniel

The first child was a girl. We named her Cheri Faith Laverne. Cheri came from the song, Ma Cheri Amour, that was co-written and performed by the great Stevie Wonder. It means "my dear love". Faith represented our trust in God that he'd keep her and Laverne is her mother's middle name.

We named our firstborn son Faithon Jemahl Glen. Faithon is "on faith" turned around, again implying our trust in God for his life. Jemahl represented the African name I always liked and Glen is my middle name.

The youngest son was named Terrance Victor Lovelton. Terrance was the name I used in my editorial column when I was editor of the campus newspaper during college. I didn't think the name Terry was all that cool, so I used Terrance for my column's heading of Terrance's Turf. Victor is one letter short of victory, implying our trust that God would give victory in his life and Lovelton is a derivative of love. When you put his two middle names together they mean "victory love".

Hebrew Boys Names Changed

The importance and significance of names in Biblical times is the reason the next thing Nebuchadnezzar did after changing the eating habits of the Hebrew youth was to command that their names be changed.

He understood that changing their names meant he essentially would be changing the core of who they were. Consequently, changing their names would be the ultimate coup d'etat or takeover. It would be the final blow in his effort to totally wipe out the Hebrew children's memory of who they were and where they'd come from.

Changing their names would also be the final humiliation for the Hebrew children and their God because in Bible days, the names children were given had reference and relationship to the God their parents served.

I've already mentioned that the name Moses means "drawn from the water". There are many other examples as well, such as: Enoch, dedicated; Abraham, father of a multitude; Jacob, supplanter; David, beloved; Solomon, peaceful; Isaiah, salvation of Jehovah; Peter, a rock; and Jonah, dove.

The parents of Hananiah, Mishael, Azariah and Daniel fully recognized the importance of the names they would give their sons and made sure their names honored their great God Jehovah.

There have been many sermons preached, Bible classes taught and songs sung about these four Hebrew boys. Virtually everyone who has ever set foot in a church has heard the story about Shadrach, Meshach and Abednego being put into the fiery furnace, or about Daniel being thrown into the lion's den.

But it's kind of strange very few people talk about how the names Shadrach, Meshach and Abednego were names given to these three lads by the prince of the eunuchs of the wicked Babylonian monarch Nebuchadnezzar. In order for them to enter the king's service, they needed to have Babylonian citizenship which was accomplished by them being given Babylonian names.

Ever since I discovered what Shadrach, Meshach and Abednego's true, God-given names were, I stopped referring to them in that manner and started using their real names.

Let's look at their real names and what they mean and you'll understand why.

Jehovah is gracious

Shadrach's God-given name is Hananiah, which means Jehovah is gracious. It reflects the attribute of God that all of us desperately need, and that is grace. If it had not been for the grace of God, all of us would have perished in our sins. But it was his grace, or unmerited favor, that prevented us from being destroyed before we had the chance to surrender our lives to him.

It was the grace of God that held back the death sentence satan pronounced upon all of us when we were rebellious teenagers. And it is that same grace that is keeping the devil from thoroughly destroying the lives of our young people today.

The Bible in the book of Ephesians, chapter two and verse eight states *"for by grace ye are saved through faith; and that not of yourselves: it is the gift of God: not of works, lest any man should boast"*.

The Hebrews were intimately familiar with how the grace of God also was what held God himself back from destroying the children of Israel. It was his grace that time and time again came to their rescue after they had been disobedient and needed deliverance from the hand of their enemies.

Chapter 16: Mpingo Jua, Hananiah, Mishael, Azariah, and Daniel

But look at what Nebuchadnezzar did in his wily attempt to wipe the memory of God's grace out of Hananiah's life. Nebuchadnezzar knew that every time Hananiah thought of his name, he was reminded of the excellent grace God had bestowed upon his people Israel.

Obviously, that was the last thing Nebuchadnezzar wanted. Consequently, Hananiah's name was changed to Shadrach, which means the command of Aku, the moon god worshipped by the heathenistic Babylonians.

Nebuchadnezzar wanted Hananiah to think about a false god, an idol god, a god that represented something the true and living God had created —the moon.

Early people thought the moon was a powerful god or goddess. The ancient Romans called their moon goddess Diana. She was the goddess of the hunt and used a moon crescent for a bow and moon beams for arrows.

The moon goddess of the ancient Greeks was Selena, and the early Egyptians honored the moon god they called Kihonsu. The Babylonians also knew the moon as Sin, sometimes called Nannan, the most powerful of the sky gods *(World Book Encyclopedia)*.

But God never intended for the people he created to worship anything other than him, as Jesus emphatically declared to satan in Matthew 4:10: *". . . for it is written, Thou shalt worship the Lord thy God, and him only shalt thou serve"*.

And when man decides to worship something other than God, there's a heavy price to be paid, as the great Apostle Paul recorded in Romans 1:21-23.

"Because that when they knew God, they glorified him not as God, neither were thankful, but became vain in their imaginations, and their foolish heart was darkened.

"Professing themselves to be wise, they became fools, and changed the glory of the uncorruptible God into an image made like to corruptible man, and to birds and four-footed beasts, and creeping things."

Who is equal to God?

In similar manner, Mishael was given the name Meshach. Mishael means "who is equal to God?" It's a name that reflects the supreme sovereignty of Almighty God. It reflects the fact that there is no one, in heaven nor in earth, who can compare with the "true and living God". It sets forth the eternal fact that God is the creator of all things, that there is none like him.

Listen to what God said about himself in Isaiah 40:25-26.

"To whom then will ye liken me, or shall I be equal? Saith the Holy One. Lift up your eyes on high, and behold who hath created these things, that bringeth out their host by number: he calleth them all by names by the greatness of his might, for that he is strong in power; not one faileth."

Or how about this in Isaiah 46:9-10.

"Remember the former things of old: for I am God, and there is none else; I am God, and there is none like me, declaring the end from the beginning, and from ancient times the things that are not yet done, saying, My counsel shall stand, and I will do all my pleasure:"

But in true satanic form, Nebuchadnezzar tried his best to eliminate the sovereignty of God out of Mishael's life. His prince of the eunuchs ordered that his name be changed to Meshach, which means "the shadow of the prince" or "who is this?"

By changing Mishael's name to Meshach, Nebuchadnezzar was attempting to black out or blot out of Mishael's mind the fact that no one could compare with God. Nebuchadnezzar wanted Mishael to relate to shadows and questions about who God was and more importantly who he was concerning God.

The devil operates the same way today. He wants to make young people completely forget about their need of God and live in a world of shadows where they hang out in dark dives and dens in the wee hours of the night, where they're confused about who they are and what life is truly all about.

He wants them to wander aimlessly through their lives trying to figure out the true meaning of life. That's why young people are so inquisitive, so willing to try different things. They've got a huge void or space of blackness in their lives that they are desperately searching to fill.

They end up using drugs, alcohol, thrills, illicit sex and other temporary fixes that cause them to continue going back to a well that just doesn't completely satisfy.

Chapter 16: Mpingo Jua, Hananiah, Mishael, Azariah, and Daniel

Jehovah hath helped

Azariah was given the name Abednego. The name Azariah means "Jehovah hath helped". The name points to the fact that God is *"a very present help in the time of trouble"* (Psalms 46:1). It refers to God's constant vigilance when it comes to watching out for his people.

"Because thou hast made the Lord, which is my refuge, even the most High, thy habitation; there shall no evil befall thee, neither shall any plague come nigh thy dwelling.

"For he shall give his angels charge over thee, to keep thee in all thy ways. They shall bear thee up in their hands, lest thou dash thy foot against a stone." (Psalms 91:9-12)

David may have said it best in Psalms 23:1-4. *"The Lord is my shepherd; I shall not want. He maketh me to lie down in green pastures; He leadeth me beside still waters, He restoreth my soul. He leadeth me in the paths of righteousness for his name's sake. Yea, though I walk through the valley of the shadow of death, I will fear no evil; for thou art with me; thy rod and thy staff they comfort me."*

But Nebuchadnezzar didn't want Azariah to remember that God was always there to watch out for him and to help him in his times of need. That's why the prince of the eunuchs changed his name to Abednego, which means Servant of Nego.

Nego was the heathen god of wisdom or the morning star. Nego was the false god the Babylonians worshiped and looked to for help and guidance. Nego was a god like all other false, heathen idols.

According to Psalms 115:4-7, *"Their idols are silver and gold, the work of men's hands. They have mouths, but they speak not: eyes have they, but they see not: they have ears, but they hear not: noses have they, but they smell not: they have hands, but they handle not: feet have they, but they walk not: neither speak they through their throat."*

What about Daniel?

I've always found it interesting that people typically refer to Hananiah, Mishael and Azariah by the heathen names they were given. On the other hand, no one refers to Daniel by his heathen name, even though all four had their names changed at the same time.

Maybe it's because Daniel authored his prophetical book about end-time occurrences. But regardless of the reason, Daniel was given a heathen name just like his friends. King Nebuchadnezzar made the same attempt, as he did with the others, to strip him of his Godly identity by having the prince of the eunuchs change his name to Belteshazzar.

The name Daniel means "God is my judge" and Nebuchadnezzar didn't like that and didn't accept the God of the Hebrews being the ultimate judge of the earth. In his paganistic thinking, the king of the land was the judge. The king made the decisions. The king was the one to be worshipped.

After all, wasn't it the Hebrews themselves who decided they didn't want the Lord to reign over them? Wasn't it the Israeli elders who boldly went to Samuel and said *"Behold, thou art old, and thy sons walk not in thy ways: now make us a king to judge us like all the nations"*. (I Samuel 8:5)

That could be why Nebuchadnezzar felt he was well within his rights as a king to demand that the people bow down and worship his image. He felt he should be the ultimate judge.

So he changed Daniel's name to Belteshazzar, which means "may Bel protect his life". Bel is also and more often spelled "Baal" in the Bible. It appears numerous times in the Old Testament with a variety of meanings such as lord, possessor, master or owner. Usually though it refers to the farm god of the Phoenicians and Canaanites, responsible for crops and flocks.

Each locality had its own Baal. The Baalim (the plural of Baal) were worshiped on high places with lascivious rites, self-torture and human sacrifice.

If you hadn't recognized it, figuratively speaking, many Baalim still exist today. They come in the forms of money, fame, sex, drugs and alcohol, new-age religions and even the way people identify themselves.

And, these modern-day Baalim are running rampant throughout our world. They've set themselves up as lords or masters over the lives of youth the world over. They have taken possession of way too many of them and have made them into puppets they're wickedly manipulating and walking them right over the edge of a cliff to hell.

It is our jobs as parents to do everything within our God-given power to prevent this from happening. In effect, we have to go to "war" with the devil to save our children from destruction.

Nebuchadnezzar Is After My Child

Chapter 17

Parents Have To Go To War!

"And, ye fathers, provoke not your children to wrath: but bring them up in the nurture and admonition of the Lord."

~ Luke 6:4

So what does it mean for parents to go to "war" with the devil on behalf of their children? What is a parents' ultimate role in helping defend their children from the all-out attack of satan? What can a parent do to prevent the devil from stealing their children's dreams, of killing their ambitions, of destroying their souls?

The first and most important thing parents can do is follow the Biblical instruction to *"train up a child in the way he should go, and when he is old he will not depart from it"* (Proverbs 22:6). God has given all parents—whether saved or unsaved—the responsibility to train their children in the fear and admonition of the Lord.

This obligation was first given to the children of Israel after the Lord delivered them out of bondage in the land of Egypt. The initial instruction God gave them after their exodus was to set apart or sanctify the firstborn child to the service of the Lord. *(Exodus 13:2)*

The purpose behind the firstborn being set apart was to remind the Israelites of how God had saved them when the death angel swept through the land of Egypt, killing all the firstborn children of the Egyptians, as well as those of the Israelis who ignored the warning to put the blood of a slain lamb upon their door posts.

The second thing the Israeli parents had to do was *"redeem"* or buy back their children by paying a price. In the case of the Israelis, God required them to *"set apart unto the Lord all that openeth the matrix (womb), and every firstling that cometh of a beast which thou hast, the males shall be the Lords"*. (Exodus 13:12)

I believe the type of redeeming or buying back of children by the Israelis means for us today that we have to sacrifice ourselves for the sake of our children. We have to pay a price for their safety, a price for them to find harmony with God.

The price is time. It's effort. It's blood. It's sweat. It's tears. It's giving our lives as an investment in our children. It's spending time with them. It's helping them with their homework. It's taking them fishing. It's coaching their basketball team, their football team. It's taxiing them back and forth to science club, chess club, drama club, ballet, track practice and other positive activities they may be involved in.

It's waiting an hour after the Friday night football game is over while your son or daughter practices with the band for the next competition. It's sitting through a perpetual downpour or 18 degree weather during the latter part of their football season. It's waiting in the high school parking lot an hour after you've gotten back from an away game for the team bus to arrive, and then another half hour for your son to get in and out of the locker room.

It's not just dropping them off at the movie theater. It's often staying at the theater while they're there, even if you watch a movie different from the one they came to see.

Paying the price to redeem your child means getting in your car when they've stayed out beyond their curfew, and driving up and down the streets of your city until you find them.

It means getting to know the friends your children hang out with, getting to know what kind of family situation those friends have and even getting to know the parents of those friends.

It's getting involved in the Parent Teacher Association (PTA) or serving as a volunteer at your child's school. It's attending the parent-child breakfast or lunch the school sponsors from time-to-time. It's doing as much as you can to be intimately involved in your child's or children's life.

Yes! It's a big price that has to be paid. It requires you to spend less time on the things you like or want to do. Sometimes you might have to go into work a little late or leave a little early, even if it means you won't impress the "boss" as much as you'd like.

But when you're willing to pay the price, it's worth every ounce of effort, every prayer that's prayed.

Chapter 17: Parents Have To Go To War!

Paying the price means *"laying down your life"* for your child. I take this from the scripture that says *"greater love hath no man than this than that a man should lay down his life for his friend"*. (St. John 15:13)

And I say it because I did it. Was I perfect? No. Did my children turn out perfect? No. But do I have any regrets that I did the best I possibly could do as far as investing myself in my children? A resounding no! No. I don't have any regrets, even when I think about the times I felt I didn't have much of a life of my own.

I did it because I'd vowed during the years I was growing up that I wouldn't do like my Father did me. My father was gone all the time. When he wasn't working or sleeping, he was usually out on the town doing "his thing".

I rarely saw him.

Granted, my father had ten kids to support, and he was always working two or three jobs at a time to make ends meet. Yes, we did always have food on the table. And we always started the school year with several changes of new clothes and a new pair of shoes to wear.

My father also taught us how to work hard. He helped us make money to buy clothes by securing us work during the summers at the estate of the wealthy man whose property he took care of or at the banks and barbershops that he cleaned on weekends or after hours.

But the thing I missed was the emotional part of a father-son relationship. I missed having someone to talk to about the issues of growing up. I needed someone to advise me, to counsel me, to coach me.

When I was playing little league baseball or junior high basketball, I wanted to look up and see my Dad in the stands, like many of the other kids were able to do. I wanted to have somebody rooting for me and pushing me to do my best. But I didn't have that with my father.

So I vowed that if I ever had children, I would be there for them, that I would give my all to be the best father to them I could be.

But as a Christian, there was another very important reason I did it. I did it because I knew that was what Jesus required me to do as a parent.

Jesus laid down his life to redeem us from the bondage of sin because he loved and loves us. So why should it be such a big thing for us to lay our lives down for our children, if we really love them?

The answer is really very simple. Many of us are just too self-absorbed, too selfish or self-centered to give up the things we like to do for the sake of spending time with our children.

Unfortunately, 20th and 21st century parents too often have not been and are not willing to pay the price of giving themselves as an investment in their children. They are too concerned about themselves, about their own goals and dreams, about their careers, about making enough money to buy that new house or new car.

But how many children have reported that the big house and luxury car didn't matter all that much to them. What they really wanted was for their parents to spend time with them.

Youth need to know where they came from
The next thing God obligated the Israelis to was to constantly remind their children of how God delivered them out of bondage.

"And it shall be when thy son asketh thee in time to come, saying, What is this? That thou shalt say unto him, by strength of hand the Lord brought us out from Egypt, from the house of bondage: And it shall be for a token upon thine hand, and for frontlets between thine eyes: for by strength of hand the Lord brought us forth out of Egypt." (Exodus 13:14 & 16)

What happened to the times in September, when life was young and oh so mellow? What happened to the spirit of commitment parents used to have for their children? What happened to the parent who did the best they could at being the kind of example God instructed them to be?

How many of today's parents have taken on the attitude that it's more important to be their child's friend than it is to be their parent, thinking that's the only way to reach them. I don't disagree that a parent needs to have a good relationship with their children and that children need to be able to talk or communicate with their parents.

What I do disagree with is the attitude that many parents have nowadays that it's necessary to *be like* their children in order to relate to them. How many of today's parents are dressing like their children, talking slang like their children, behaving like their children and in effect being their children?

Chapter 17: Parents Have To Go To War!

Something is desperately wrong when the youth are setting the fashion and behavioral trends for adults. Remember Allen Iverson? He's the former professional basketball player for the Philadelphia 76ers. When he was drafted into the league, he quickly gained a reputation for having a rebellious attitude, multitude of tattoos and promoting profanity-laced rap lyrics. Iverson, despite being one of the NBA's greatest and most entertaining players, was often roundly criticized for his gansta-style antics.

But like most people, when we get older and feel like we've let some opportunities slip from our grasp, we start soul-searching the reason it happened. That's why when Iverson had gotten older and wiser and recognized the opportunities he'd forfeited, he finally admitted in a USA Today article just before the 2001 All-Star game that "it's time to grow up".

God expects all of us to grow to adulthood. He expects all of us to shed the irresponsible attitude and behavior of our youth and take on the responsibility of adulthood.

Since God created us, he fully understands that it takes time for children to mature. He well knows that children will make mistakes that often will cause them to fall on their faces. He knows how impressionable they are and how it often takes them running into walls before they get the message.

How many of us adults still have mental and physical scars to remind us of how irresponsible we were in our younger years? You don't have to raise your hands.

But God also knows there comes a time when a child has to grow up. There comes a time when that child has to start accepting adult responsibilities, when that child has to put away their Nintendos, Game Boys, PlayStations, Wiis and Xboxes and step out into the world as a man or a woman.

Paul emphatically asserted *"when I was a child I spake as a child, I understood as a child, I thought as a child; but when I became a man, I put away childish things"*. (I Corinthians 13:11)

My children often got on my case about how I carried myself when they were growing up. They called me a nerd. They told me I wasn't stylish enough. They said I needed to loosen up.

What they were really saying is "Dad, you ought to be like us. That's the way to be cool".

Thank God, I didn't fall into that trap. I stood my ground. The reason is that if I had lowered my standards to theirs, I would have in effect been lowering my standards to those of a child.

Whenever a parent projects a juvenile image to their children, it hurts them. It means they have no role model before them. It means they don't have anything to ascend to. It means they don't have to look at being better, to look at growing up and putting childish things away. It means they can remain a child forever.

Wasn't that what Peter Pan wanted, to be a child forever? And didn't the book and movies spawn a following of children—myself included for a while—who thought they could escape to Neverland and never have to grow up.

Michael Jackson, arguably the greatest performer of all-time, tried that too. Listen to what renowned poet, cultural critic, syndicated columnist and novelist Stanley Crouch wrote about Jackson in a 2009 column:

"As a man who was never able to be an actual child because he became too famous too soon, Jackson seemed to maintain a determined nostalgia for what he had not experienced. Part of his trouble was that he became wealthy enough to create his own world of perpetual childhood.

"The character Michael Jackson often resembled as the plastic surgery operations continued to slice and remake him was actually the Walt Disney version of Peter Pan. That personally chosen look was periodically upgraded with one nip and tuck after another . . ."

Jackson even named the famous ranch he lived at after Neverland, the fantasy island in the story of Peter Pan. According to various news reports, the Neverland Ranch contained an amusement park, petting zoo and various other children attractions.

Unfortunately, the world isn't a fantasy place where children don't have to grow up. God's plan has always been for us to grow up, to take on the responsibilities of adulthood. He never intended for anyone to wander aimlessly in a never, never land where they never grow old—at least not down here on planet earth.

Chapter 17: Parents Have To Go To War!

God's intent is that adults—mothers and fathers—teach their young men and women to grow up to be sober-minded and live lives that are patterns of good works.

A pattern is defined by Webster's Dictionary as *"the regular and repeated way in which something happens or is done"* or *"something that happens in a regular and repeated way"*. God wants young people to live their lives in this type of manner so their peers can look up to and emulate them. He wants them to set the right kind of example for others when it comes to how God wants us to relate to him, how we relate to our parents, our spouses and to each other.

Look at what Titus, chapter 2, verses 1 through 8 says.

"But speak thou the things which become sound doctrine: that the aged men be sober, grave, temperate, sound in faith, in charity, in patience. The aged women likewise, that they be in behavior as becometh holiness, not false accusers, not given to much wine, teachers of good things;

"That they may teach the young women to be sober, to love their husbands, to love their children, to be discreet, chaste, keepers at home, good, obedient to their own husbands, that the Word of God be not blasphemed.

"Young men likewise exhort to be sober minded. In all things showing thyself a pattern of good works; in doctrine showing uncorruptness, gravity, sincerity, sound speech, that cannot be condemned; that he that is of the contrary part may be ashamed, having no evil thing to say of you."

What God is setting forth in these scriptures is the role he expects parents to play. It's the example he wants parents to be for their children, and if they are not, they are doing their children a major disservice.

15 steps for good parenting

I'll be the first to say that parenting is hard work. It's filled with challenges the moment that cute baby is born. And, most of us know how the terrible two's can't compare with the tumultuous teens.

We also know that all of us are different. We are uniquely made, with distinctive personalities and physical make-ups. Consequently, parents have to be wise in their parenting styles when it comes to using the right style that works best for their children.

That's why we all can use a little help or guidance. Here's some from the Full Life Study Bible (Zondervan, KJV ©1992). It's 15 steps a parent can take to lead their child or children to a life of godliness in Christ.

1. *Dedicate your children to God at the beginning of their lives (I Samuel 1:28; Luke 2:22).*
2. *Teach your children to fear the Lord and turn away from evil, to love righteousness and to hate iniquity (Hebrews 1:9).*
3. *Teach your children to obey you as parents through Biblical discipline (Deuteronomy 8:5; Proverbs 3:11-12; 13:24).*
4. *Protect your children from ungodly influences by being aware of satan's attempts to destroy them spiritually through attraction to the world or through immoral companions (Proverbs 13:20; 28:7; I John 2:15-17).*
5. *Make your children aware that God is always observing and evaluating what they do, think, and say (Psalms 139:1-12).*
6. *Bring your children early in life to personal faith, repentance and water baptism in Christ (Matthew 19:14).*
7. *Establish your children in a spiritual church where God's word is proclaimed. His righteous standards honored and the Holy Spirit is manifested (Psalms 1119:63).*
8. *Encourage your children to remain separated from the world and to witness and work for God (II Corinthians 6:14-7:1).*
9. *Instruct them in the importance of the baptism in the Holy Spirit (Acts 1:4-5, 8; 2:4,39).*
10. *Teach your children that God loves them and has a specific purpose for their lives (Luke 1:13-17; Romans 8:29-30).*
11. *Instruct your children daily in the sacred scriptures, both in conversation and family devotions (Deuteronomy 4:9; 6:5-7; II Timothy 3:15).*
12. *Through example and exhortation, encourage your children to devote themselves to prayer (Acts 6:4; Romans 12:12; Ephesians 6:18).*
13. *Prepare your children to suffer and endure persecution for the sake of righteousness (Matthew 5:10-12).*
14. *Lift your children up to God by constant and fervent intercession (Ephesians 6:18; James 5:16).*

Chapter 17: Parents Have To Go To War!

15. Have such love and concern for your children that you would be willing to pour out your life as if it were a sacrifice unto the Lord, in order to deepen their faith and make their lives what they should be in the Lord (Philippians 2:17).

Wait a minute. Let me say it for you. These 15 steps are much easier said than done. I will be the first to acknowledge that. It is extremely difficult to execute these ideas because it requires the cooperation of children who don't always—all right most always—don't want to cooperate.

It takes a very wise and extremely patient parent to effectively instill the Godly principles in their children that will be cemented in their hearts, minds and souls for the rest of their lives.

Because it is so hard, and because children will make mistakes, I believe parents can help their children survive the tumultuous and dangerous years of their youth by teaching them the simple principles I tried my best to deeply plant within my children.

So what are those principles, and how can young people cope in a world that has turned into what the Temptations prophetically described in the 70's as "a ball of confusion".

How can they cope in a world gone mad, where Godly morals, values and standards barely exist anymore and have been replaced by the so-called political correctness of diversity and tolerance which largely goes against everything God has commanded when it comes to living.

Simply put, youth have got to be SMART.

Nebuchadnezzar Is After My Child

Part IV

I Am Come That You Might Have Life

Nebuchadnezzar Is After My Child

Chapter 18

Youth Have Got To Be **SMART**

"My son, hear the instructions of thy father, and forsake not the law of thy mother: for they shall be an ornament of grace unto thy head, and chains about thy neck."

~ Proverbs 1:8-9

When it comes to being smart, I'm not talking about the aspect of being smart—in the intellectual sense—that most of us typically relate to. I'm not talking about how high a person's IQ (intelligence quotient) is. I'm using SMART as an acronym for being: **S**ingle-**M**inded, **A**lert, **R**esolute and **T**enacious.

God opened up my eyes to the importance of young people being **SMART** in this manner during the time my children were in their their middle and high school years. It seemed that as soon as they hit these years that everything I had learned about parenting was no longer relevant.

Suddenly, all the wisdom and knowledge I'd gained while they were pre-teens didn't apply to the issues and challenges they and I were now confronted with. And it became a day-by-day learning situation all over again.

It was also during this time when I was seeing more clearly how the devil was wreaking havoc among young people everywhere, those who were being reared in church and those who were not receiving any church upbringing.

The principles were really crystallized following several situations involving my oldest son, Faithon. Faithon was very smart intellectually. Academics came easy for him. He was the type who didn't have to study hard to make good grades. He graduated Who's Who in High School and received a college scholarship to play football.

But despite my best efforts at trying to instill good, common sense into him, he didn't seem to get it. Consequently, he experienced what I'll call several mental lapses during his middle and high school years that left me asking God what more could I do to help him be smarter about keeping himself out of trouble.

The first mental mistake Faithon made occurred during his Freshman year. While it's very unlikely that I'll ever know the full truth about what happened, my son was allegedly spotted by a teacher either "taking a roach out of another student's hand or putting it into the other student's hand".

Just in case you don't know, I'm not talking about the insect type of cockroach, although I do detest the sight of the pest. I wish I were. That would have made things a lot easier for me to deal with. But it wasn't as simple as buying a can of insect spray.

The kind of roach I'm talking about is the "butt" or "end" of a marijuana cigarette or "joint" that smokers usually dispose of. Marijuana roaches are usually about a quarter-inch long, the part of the joint that's held between the thumb and index finger.

The teacher, who was standing in a door-way about 20 feet away, said she really couldn't tell if the other student was placing the roach "into" my son's hand or taking it "out" of his hand.

Here's my son's story. He was on his way to gym class. In order to get to the gym, he had to walk outside from one wing of the school to the other side where the gym was located. While en route, he saw another student, a senior whom he didn't know from Adam, bend down and pick up something from off the ground.

He thought, "let me go see what he got". As his story goes, the older student had picked up the roach off the ground and they were examining it when the teacher spotted them from the doorway.

No other trace of marijuana was found on either student, but by having the illegal substance in their possession, they were in violation of school rules. In fact, possession of marijuana was a crime, so the police had to be called in.

Well, after exhausting the appeal process, both boys were expelled from school for the remainder of the year. And, I ended up having to spend several hundred dollars a month to send Faithon to private school.

Chapter 18: Youth Have Got To Be SMART

The kicker came when Faithon got expelled a second time his junior year in high school. That expulsion occurred after a teacher claimed to have spotted him and one of his good friends passing a substance back and forth. The teacher was a fair distance away and couldn't tell exactly what they had, but alleged it was some type of drug.

The teacher went out and confronted the boys, who claimed they didn't have any drugs. And, even though the teacher didn't find anything on them, she insisted they had to have had something. She subsequently, marched the boys to the principles office where they were searched and nothing was found at that time either. Nevertheless, they were suspended from the school.

Now mind you, both my son and his friend excelled academically and were both members of the football team. They both had saved parents who were raising them in church and diligently teaching them Godly principles. But, here they were, accused of passing an illegal substance back and forth and expelled from school.

It put the boys' futures in jeopardy and caused me and the parents of my son's friend to spend money sending them to private school.

"Boy," I found myself constantly reminding him, "you gotta be smart. You just can't be doing things that end up getting you in trouble. Life is much too difficult as it is than for you to bring things upon yourself. You gotta be smarter than that."

I tried to explain to him that being smart meant:
- knowing how to avoid trouble.
- learning how not to hang around with negative influences or the wrong people.
- knowing how to leave a party when someone brought out drugs or alcohol.
- knowing how to diffuse an argument or walk away prior to a fight escalating.
- not going to watch a fight, no matter if everyone else planned to do so.
- not following the crowd, or feeling like you have to be like everybody else.

- knowing how to respect young ladies and understanding sex should be confined to marriage.
- recognizing the importance of making good grades throughout school and pursuing higher education or a good trade that would let you make a decent living.
- and most of all, it meant realizing the importance of having God in your life so He could direct your life's path.

And "blink" the light went on. It was at that moment the idea for "You Gotta Be SMART" was born. It was a motivational youth program designed to educate young people about the perils that surrounded them, the potential pitfalls they would encounter, the challenges they would face, and most of all, how the devil was out to destroy them, based on how the wicked king Nebuchadnezzar tried his best to destroy Daniel, Hananiah, Mishael and Azariah.

Being **S**ingle-**M**inded, **A**lert, **R**esolute and **T**enacious are principles that I strongly believe can help a young person, in partnership with their parents, successfully navigate themselves through the tumultuous storms of life and escape the multitude of traps set for them by the devil.

Let's look at each principle individually.

Chapter 19

You've Got To Be Single-Minded

"As the hart panteth after the water brooks, so panteth my soul after thee O God."

~ Psalms 42:1

Having **S**ingle-**M**indedness means having or concentrating on only one aim or purpose. It means being determined, committed, unswerving, unwavering, purposeful, uncompromising and tireless. It means being completely focused on the task or goal at hand.

However, **S**ingle-**M**indedness is something modern-day young people seem to have great difficulty with. It's hard for them to concentrate on one thing at a time. It's hard for them to see things through. But in order to successfully make it in life, they must learn to exercise this principle.

Paul said in Philippians 3:14 & 14 *"Brethren, I count not myself to have apprehended: but this one thing I do, forgetting those things which are behind, and reaching forth unto those things which are before, I press toward the mark for the prize of the high calling of God in Christ Jesus."*

The message Paul was giving in this text was about the necessity of being laser-focused on reaching the goal of making it to Heaven. But in doing so, he also was describing the process required for successfully reaching any goal or driving for any dream and not letting anything interfere with realizing it.

Single-**M**indedness is having complete focus on a goal like Paul described. It's being able to see things through to the end.

It means being able to properly deal with distractions, such as a friend calling to talk on the phone, or someone dropping by to see if you want to go out for some fun, or anything else that would take you away from a task you're trying to complete.

It means maintaining interest on the things that are most important in life and to your future.

This type of **S**ingle-**M**indedness is lacking among too many of our young people, due to a variety of reasons related to living in modern society.

Have you recently heard your child complain about being "bored"? That's because they have difficulty sitting still for any length of time. They can't stand dealing with the same thing very long. Their attention span is very limited.

Our children and grandchildren live in the age of progress and technology. They were born into a fast-paced society where they don't have to wait on anything.

They are used to fast food burgers. They're used to "surfing" cable channels on widescreen televisions. They're used to getting information from anywhere in the world by pressing a few keys and manipulating a "mouse" via the information super highway, better known as the Internet.

Our children live in the age of telecommunications. They're used to walking around with cell phones, iPods or iPads where they're continuously connected with their friends, music, games and movies.

As a matter of fact, many of our young people today aren't even familiar with what we older folks know as land-line phones. They communicate with their cell phones via talk, text and FaceTime and over the Internet via social media like Facebook, Twitter, Snapchat, Instagram or some of the other popular ones discussed in Chapter 14.

According to The Statistics Portal found on statista, which provides statistics and study results from 18,000 sources, as of February 2016, "93 percent of teens ages 15-17 have mobile access to the internet through a phone, tablet or other device[11].

"In North America, young adults and teenagers aged 16-24 spend the most time online via mobile, more than any other age group, spending nearly 200 minutes per day on a mobile device[12]. That's three hours and 20 minutes of their time.

"Teen and Millennial age groups now spend almost as much time on mobile devices as they do on a PC/laptop/tablet[13]. Among high school graduates, when on their mobile devices, the most popular social networks and apps include text messaging, followed by Instagram, then Facebook and Snapchat[14]."

Chapter 19: You've Got To Be Single-Minded

Our young people are accustomed to fast-paced video games where they can move from one level or "life" to another within minutes and compete on the internet with other players from around the world.

Unlike us baby boomers who have had to adjust to rapid change and state of the art technology, today's young people are used to and very comfortable with constant and rapid change. High tech gadgets have always been a normal part of their lives, and the overwhelming result of it all is their attention span has been reduced to mere minutes, seconds or sound bytes.

I first began noticing this difference in attention span in today's young people with my youngest son, who is in his 30's now and plays video games with his own sons.

Initially, I didn't understand why he was having more difficulty in school than his two older siblings. I had a hard time with why he couldn't seem to get his homework done very well—until the Spirit of God revealed it to me one day.

Squirt, as we've always called him, was a product of the computer generation. He was a product of the video game age, the age of video arcades that got jump-started by a funny, yellow-colored ball with bug eyes called Pac Man.

I noticed that when it came to playing video games, Squirt didn't have any problem at all completely absorbing himself in the game. I noticed how excited Squirt became while playing the games. I noticed how proficient Squirt became at playing the games. I noticed how Squirt could maintain his attention on these games for long periods of time, if we let him.

But at the same time, I noticed that Squirt didn't seem to be able to focus as well when it came to reading a book or doing his homework. It was just too slow and boring to capture his full attention.

As I observed this, my eyes began to open. Squirt was born into the age of technology and speed. He was a product of the times.

Goals must be specific

Similar to Squirt when he was a teenager, many of today's teens grapple with focus. They far too often get distracted from the things that will have the most positive impact on their lives and fall into traps that have been set for them by the devil.

That's why in order for young people to be the best they can be and avoid satan's pitfalls and snares, it's essential they learn to exercise the principle of **Single-M**indedness, particularly as it relates to knowing what they want out of life and going after it with all they've got. Young people must learn how to have a purpose and how to set goals in life. And, that goal or purpose has to be *specific*.

I'll never forget the time I was addressing a group of minority students at a college in my hometown. One of the students was a young lady who attended the same church I did and I knew her pretty well. As I went around the room asking the students what they were majoring in, this sister replied "general studies".

My immediate question to her was "what kind of job do you expect to get with a major in general studies?" I asked the question very tactfully because I didn't want to offend the sister. But I felt it was important to make the point that even when it comes to going to college, you have to set specific goals, which in turn means you have to know specifically what major is required to meet that goal.

Obviously, the sister had no answer regarding the type of work she could get with a general studies major. And, unfortunately for her, she hasn't fared as well in life as she would have liked. I'm not aware that she ever did get a degree and she's bounced around from job to job. It seems that she just never could stay focused on her prize.

The moral of the story is a degree in general studies just couldn't cut it then, and it definitely won't cut it in today's super competitive world.

Did I know what I wanted to be when I was growing up? Not by any means! Both my parents were uneducated. There was never talk in our household about goals and careers. There was no talk about college or pursuing a profession.

Chapter 19: You've Got To Be Single-Minded

All we were encouraged to do was finish high school and get a job in a factory, like everyone else we knew did. After all, factory jobs were plentiful in the 60's, 70's and even into the 80's".

The only thing I thought I wanted to do was to go somewhere to play football. I knew the next level to do that was in college, but I didn't know how to get there and I had no mentor to advise me. Consequently, it was just a dream lodged in the recesses of my mind.

Even after I ended up in college, the story of which is told in *"Looking For A Place In The Sun"*, I didn't know what I wanted to be. That's why I started out majoring in physical education. To me that was logical since I had been an athlete in high school. I thought maybe I could become a gym teacher.

But then after having a deep discussion about the woes and issues of society with my roommate and other friends, I changed my major to sociology. I felt as an African-American who was dedicated to the "movement", it was somewhat my obligation to help change the world and make things better for us all.

But that was short-lived also, after I found out about the low wages and long, hot hours social workers were subjected to.

So, I started thinking about philosophy. Since I read so many books and was very cerebral, I thought maybe I could become a thinker, someone who philosophized about life. Even though it was my belief at the time that philosophers really didn't do anything substantial, at least you had a good thought on the subject of life.

Thank God, that He was watching out for me and He's the one who maneuvered me into the field of journalism and communications. If not for that who knows where I might have ended up?

Even though God finally steered me straight, I lost of lot of time through high school and college wandering and wondering. I had no specific goals and wasted a lot of precious time that I could have been using to learn and hone the skills necessary to be successful in life.

The important point of the matter is, for young people to steer clear of the numerous traps of the devil, they need to have specific goals and be determined to pursue them with everything they've got.

Goals must be realistic

Goals also have to be *realistic*. Young people have to recognize their limitations. I've used the example many times about the thousands of young men who wanted to be the next Michael Jordan or the next Kobe Bryant, and now the next Stephen Curry, LeBron James or Kevin Durant.

It's fine to want to be a great basketball player, but if you only grow to be five-foot, eight inches tall and can't even touch the rim, then it's really not a very realistic goal to think you're going to become a millionaire basketball player.

Besides, according to NCAA (National Collegiate Athletic Association) research, more than 480,000 compete as NCAA athletes, and just a select few within each sport move on to compete at the professional or Olympic level. Slightly more than 1 percent (1.1 percent) make it to men's professional basketball and 0.9 percent make it to women's professional basketball.

And, if you think the odds of making it to the professional level is any better in football or baseball, think again. The NCAA research notes that only 1.6 percent make it to men's professional football, and only 9.9 percent make it to men's professional baseball.

On the other hand, there are many opportunities that exist in the fields of education, communications, medicine, science, technology, engineering and math (STEM) that are available for young people to pursue. These fields don't require that a person stand six-foot-six or more, or run a 4.5 forty-yard-dash. All they require is a willingness to study hard.

Need to recognize our limitations

Being **S**ingle-**M**inded also means being able to *recognize your limitations*. It means knowing what field of study best suits you. Yes, while opportunities abound in STEM fields, if you don't have the aptitude for math or science, pursue the area of study that you enjoy and do have the capabilities for.

The young lady who was majoring in general studies is also a good example of a person who didn't recognize their limitations. While she was a capable choir singer, the sister always insisted that she wanted to be a

Chapter 19: You've Got To Be Single-Minded

lead singer. She wanted to lead songs. In fact, I've personally heard the sister say she wanted to have a singing career.

Unfortunately, the sister just didn't have a good enough voice to be a lead singer and the choir director never allowed her to lead songs. And it stands to reason that if you're not good enough to lead a choir song, there's no reason to think a singing career is in your future.

I've wanted to be able to sing ever since I committed my life to Christ my senior year in college. Once I started attending church, it seemed that nearly everyone could sing. I even tried my hand at singing in choir several times. But the strain on my throat was just too much for me to bear. Initially, I thought the problem I had was that I hadn't gotten in church early enough to develop a good singing voice.

Eventually, I figured out that really wasn't the problem at all. I just didn't have a very good singing voice, and it just wasn't meant for me to be a singer. Was I disappointed in this revelation? Absolutely.

But I gradually came to accept the fact that the best I'd ever be able to do was lead the devotion or praise services. And as I did that with all my heart, God actually abundantly blessed me in this area. He developed me to a point where He has used me immensely over the years in the devotion or praise portions of the service to invoke the spirit of praise and worship where the people were blessed in a big way.

Have I ever had the urge to want to be a lead singer since? I certainly have. Have I ever had to fight off the spirit of jealously when it came to singing? By all means.

But I have also reached the point where when it comes to lead singing, I'm content with singing to myself, singing to my wife and singing to God. I now appreciate "my gift". I know my wife appreciates it. And I know God appreciates it.

But when it comes to sharing it with the rest of the world, I came to grips with the fact that I'll have to wait until I get to heaven and receive new "lungs" and new "vocal cords" of a heavenly nature. Then I'll be able to sing like an angel.

I can hardly wait.

Goals must be short-term and long-term

In addition to setting specific, realistic goals, and knowing your limitations, young people have to recognize that their goals should be of a *short-term and long-term nature*. I've often used the example of how to get good grades in school to illustrate short and long-term goal setting.

I learned the invaluable lesson during my first year in college that you can't end up with all A's at the end of the year by focusing all your efforts on studying the last month or last week of school. It's necessary to take it one essay at a time, one report at a time, one test at a time.

You have to focus on doing well on each individual assignment during each individual quarter or semester. Too often young people think they can coast during the bulk of the school year and then catch up at the end. Most of us don't have the intellectual horsepower to do it that way. We've got to take it one step at a time.

I use a similar example when it comes to careers. You just don't become a doctor, a lawyer or a journalist overnight. Ideally, you need to start off in grade school making good grades. Then you've got to make good grades in middle school and start taking the proper classes in the field you want to go into.

Then when you get to high school, if your chosen field is journalism, you've got to make the smart choices of taking english and writing classes, and working on the high school newspaper, radio and television stations (if they're offered).

By the time you get into college, you're well on your way to reaching the career goal that you've set for yourself. College becomes a time when you can take all the necessary courses to refine your skills and focus on being the best you can be in your given field of journalism, whether it's print, broadcast or social. It also becomes a time when you can do internships and prepare to get a job after college graduation.

It's a process of taking it one step at a time, meeting the short-term goals of making it through the quarter or semester, then half the year (mid-term exams), then the entire year (final exams). After you've met the series of short-term goals, you can suddenly wake up to the realization that your long-term goal has been achieved.

Setting realistic, specific, short- and long-term goals and recognizing your limitations and then focusing on reaching those goals. That's what it

Chapter 19: You've Got To Be Single-Minded

means to be **S**ingle-**M**inded. When young people can do this, they're well on their way to being able to achieve victory over the enemy. But it doesn't stop there. They've also got to be **A**lert.

Nebuchadnezzar Is After My Child

Chapter 20

You've Got To Be Alert

"See then that you walk circumspectly, not as fools, but as wise."

~ Ephesians 5:15

The next important aspect of being SMART is being Alert. The dictionary definition for alert is the act of being "quick to notice any unusual and potentially dangerous or difficult circumstances".

Being quick to notice potential danger or difficulty is vital for young people to successfully navigate through the maze of life's issues, particularly as it relates to the various weapons the devil uses to attack them with. They've got to be Alert to what's going on around them and the negative impact these things can potentially have on their lives.

The Biblical description for this is *"walking circumspectly"*. Ephesians 5:15 states *"see then that ye walk circumspectly, not as fools, but as wise"*. Being circumspect means thinking about possible risks or consequences before doing or saying something. It means taking into consideration all possible circumstances and consequences before acting. It means being vigilant, observant and attentive to the things going on around you.

All too often, before considering the consequences of their actions, young people tend to act impulsively. They say or do things on the spur of the moment. And, then after they do something that has a negative impact, they wonder what happened.

But, in order to successfully avoid negative pitfalls as they navigate through life, young people need to exercise circumspection or alertness when it comes to the actions they take.

A great example of how one person is helping teach young people to think before they act is a guy named Eugene Brown, an ex-convict who started the Big Chair Chess Club for inner-city youths in Washington, D.C. The story about Brown and the chess club he started is told in the movie *"Life of a King"*, starring Cuba Gooding, Jr., as Brown.

Brown, who was incarcerated 18 years, was taught the game of chess while behind bars and learned invaluable lessons from it, most importantly, the need to think before you move. It is this reasoning—thinking before you move or act—that he teaches young people through his Big Chair Chess Club.

Thinking before you move, walking circumspectly or being **A**lert is a critical life skill all young people need to have due to the myriad of challenges the devil is bombarding them with. Some of the most prominent challenges facing our youth during this new millennium have been around for a while. Others have recently emerged. But all are like giant goliaths that are relentlessly stalking our young people for the purpose of capturing them, torturing them and ultimately destroying them.

These goliaths include drug use and abuse, alcoholism, violence, violent music genres, bullying, teenage pregnancy, sexually transmitted diseases as a result of illicit sex, illiteracy, social media interaction and suicide.

Let's take a look at these goliaths individually.

Drug use and abuse

While drug use and abuse have been a problem in America for many years, it exploded in the 1960's, which was during my teenage years. It became progressively worse and in 1973 prompted President Richard Nixon's administration to create the Drug Enforcement Agency (DEA). Later, when the great college basketball player Len Bias, of the University of Maryland, died of a cocaine overdose one day after being the second player selected in the 1986 NBA draft, there was a nationwide panic about cocaine abuse. This led Nancy Reagan, wife of President Ronald Reagan, to launch her "Just Say No" to drugs campaign that same year.

This campaign, however, barely put a dent in the drug problem. The epidemic of drug use and abuse continued to spiral out of control throughout the years my children were growing up during the mid to late

Chapter 20: You've Got To Be Alert

80's and early 1990's. And, it continues to be a prominent, widespread problem in our society during the New Millennium.

The cable television mini-series entitled "The Corner" aptly illustrated how this wicked goliath preys on and destroys our young people. The mini-series aired in the year 2000 and was directed by mega movie star Charles Dutton. It was set in inner city Baltimore, MD, one of the most financially depressed areas in the nation at the time.

The series was adapted from the book *"The Corner: A Year in the Life of an Inner-City Neighborhood"* by David Simon a reporter for the Baltimore Sun for 13 years and Ed Burns, a retired Baltimore homicide detective. They wrote the book based on experience of following the toll drug addiction and crime were having on the real-life activities of economically-depressed people in a west-side Baltimore neighborhood. One of the "victims" in the mini-series was a 15-year-old boy who lost a job and saw dealing drugs as one of his few options for income.

The area in Baltimore featured in "The Corner" is an area I'm personally familiar with since I've lived in the Baltimore area twice. In fact, the last time I lived there, I participated in a volunteer work project in which I joined several colleagues to help renovate run-down row-houses in the neighborhood.

Amazingly, while performing the work, we watched prostitutes, drug pushers and drug buyers parade in broad daylight up and down the street conducting their business—the type of business that sadly was bleeding the very life out of each and every one of them.

It was very sad to watch.

It used to be that drug use and trafficking were confined to the blighted, run-down urban areas of our cities like the one in Baltimore. But that's far from the case anymore. The drug infestation has stretched its tentacles to virtually every nook and cranny of society and has taken hold on even the most up-scale and pristine suburban areas.

The movie "Traffic" cast a bright spotlight on the situation of drug use in the suburbs. "Traffic" won several Academy awards, including best picture, for movies that were released in the year 2000. The movie stars Michael Douglas as a judge who becomes the nation's new drug czar. The judge's wife has a youthful history of drugs, and his 16-year old daughter, a straight-A student at a fancy private school, starts freebasing cocaine, then turns tricks to pay for her habit.

It's a picture that's become much too common in our world. Dad, Mom and child all caught up in the vicious cycle of drug use and abuse, with the child ending up suffering the worst consequences.

Thanks to the popularity of the movie Traffic, the cover story in the February 12, 2001 issue of *Newsweek Magazine* was about the fact that while substance abuse was down, about 14 million people were still hooked on drugs and alcohol.

Newsweek reported that the movie went a long way in resurrecting the debate about the widespread abuse and effects of drugs in our society. The article noted that heroin use among teens was rising in San Francisco, Newark, N.J. and Atlanta and that so-called club drugs like ecstasy were on the rise in cities like Boston and St. Louis.

But if you think the renewed emphasis at that time on solving the drug and alcohol abuse issue helped curb the rise in drug use among young people, think again.

According to a May 2015 report by the National Institute on Drug Abuse (NIDA), 60 percent of high school seniors didn't see regular marijuana use as harmful, but THC (the active ingredient in the drug that causes addiction) is nearly five times stronger than it was 20 years ago.

- Six and a half percent of high school seniors smoked pot daily.
- Less than 20 percent of 12th graders thought occasional use was harmful, while less than 40 percent believed regular use was harmful.
- About 50 percent of high school seniors did not think it was harmful to try crack or cocaine once or twice and 40 percent believed it wasn't harmful to use heroin once or twice.

And, if consuming illegal drugs isn't bad enough, young people are dying at record rates as a result of using prescription drugs.

The NIDA reported that in 2013, more teens died from prescription drugs than heroin and cocaine combined.

Chapter 20: You've Got To Be Alert

Even worse is the abuse of drugs by middle and high school athletes in their attempt to gain an edge in sports. The NIDA said 54 percent of high school seniors did not think regular steroid use was harmful.

To compound matters even more, as of the year 2016, 25 states in America had passed laws making medical and recreational use of marijuana legal. Four of those states, and the District of Columbia, have legalized marijuana for recreational use. In Alaska, adults 21 and older can now transport, buy or possess up to an ounce of marijuana and six plants. Oregon voters approved a similar measure allowing adults to possess up to an ounce of marijuana in public and 8 ounces in their homes. Colorado and Washington previously passed similar ballot measures legalizing marijuana in 2012 *(from governing.com)*.

While marijuana has been scientifically proven to relieve pain and other symptoms, its legalization has been a boon to teenagers who want to get high. According to the NIDA: one-third of teenagers who live in the states get their pot from other people's prescriptions.

And that's only half the story, based on the state of Colorado, where various reports state that legalizing marijuana is completely backfiring—particularly in regards to the young.

According to a June 2015 opinion piece published in Newsweek Magazine as a result of Colorado legalizing weed, its use among teens has increased, resulting in educational problems in middle and high schools, a spike in "edibles"-related emergency room visits, consumption by children and pets resulting in illness and death and regulatory confusion surrounding public consumption and enforcement.

Additionally, the article said "Teen drug-related school expulsions are also on the rise.[15] And the notion that prisons filled with minor drug offenders would be relieved of overcrowding—a selling point of legalizing marijuana—has been blown to smithereens."[16]

What happened to the days of yea and nay?

In the bottle

Sadly, today's youth not only are heavily involved in drugs, they are also in the bottle.

There was a song out during my college years titled *"The Bottle"*. It was a song about the devastating social impact drinking alcoholic beverages was having on people—the alcoholics, their families, their children, their communities.

The song was released by an artist named Gil Scott Heron in 1974. Here are some lyrics to part of the song:

"See that sister, sho' was fine
Before she started drinkin' wine in a bottle
She told me her old man committed a crime
He's doin' time and now she's hangin' in a bottle
I seen her out there on the avenue
All by herself, she sho' need help from the bottle
I seen a preacher man try to help her out
She cussed him out and hit him in the head with a bottle"

Sounds a lot like today. Alcohol use and abuse are still destroying peoples' lives, tearing families apart and negatively impacting our communities.

According to the National Institute of Alcohol and Alcoholism (NIAA), in 2014 there were 16.3 adults (18 and older) who had alcohol use disorder (AUD). But the worst part is that there was an estimated 679,000 youth (ages 12-17) who had AUD. Of that number, an estimated 55,000 youth received treatment for an alcohol problem in a specialized facility in 2014.

When it comes solely to underage drinking, according to a NIAA survey on Drug Use and Health conducted in 2014, nearly 35 percent of 15-year-olds reported that they had a least one drink in their lives and about 8.7 million people ages 12 to 20 reported drinking alcohol in the past month.

Those are scary statistics, particularly when considering the consequences reported by the NIAA. It's research indicates that alcohol use during the teenage years could interfere with normal adolescent brain development and increase the risk of developing AUD. Additionally, underage drinking contributes to a range of acute consequences, including injuries, sexual assaults and even deaths, including those from car crashes.

Chapter 20: You've Got To Be Alert

Teen violence

Compounding the problem of drug and alcohol use and abuse is that teenage violence in our communities and schools is another goliath that's preying on our youth.

The issue of violence as it relates to how youth are being influenced by media was extensively discussed in chapter 13. But violence and its impact on youth extend far beyond the horror of mass shootings, as confirmed by the following statistics reported in 2010 by the Center for Disease Control (CDC) (Ad Injection:randomTeenHelp).

- 4,828 young people, ages 10-24, were victims of homicide; an average of 13 each day.
- 82.8 percent of of youth homicides were committed with a firearm.
- Juveniles under 18 accounted for 13.7 percent of all violent crime arrests and 22.5 percent of all property crime arrests.
- 784 juveniles were arrested for murder.
- 2,198 juveniles were arrested for forcible rape.
- 35,001 juveniles were arrested for aggravated assault.

Nowhere is the devastating impact of violence on our youth more pronounced than in the great city of Chicago. Look at this statement contained in the city's Youth Violence Prevention Plan presented during the National Forum on Youth Violence Prevention held in 2014.

"Children who are exposed to neighborhood violence, particularly gun violence, suffer increased rates of depression, aggression, delinquency, poor school performance, and risky sexual behavior (Jenkins et al., 2009). . . .

"Violence affects everyone in Chicago, but it is particularly devastating for our youth. In 2010, 1,109 school-aged youth were shot, and 216 of those were killed. Nearly half of Chicago's homicide victims are young people between the ages of 10 and 25. In 2009, 65 percent of all violent crime arrests were of youth 25 or younger. It is impossible to discuss violence in Chicago without addressing the youth who are so often both the perpetrators and the victims of violence."

It's a very sad state of affairs.

Music Taking Over Minds

Everyone loves music. Since the Bible days music has been a tremendously influential factor in the lives of human beings. King Saul is a great example of the affect music can have on the psyche and soul of man.

The book of I Samuel records the events surrounding Saul being anointed the first king of the nation of Israel, his initial triumphs, then his fall from grace as a result of his disobedience to God's command to utterly destroy the Amalekites (I Samuel 16). Rather than do exactly as Samuel the prophet had directed him, Saul decided to spare Agag, the Amalekite King, as well as the best of the livestock.

To make things worse, when Samuel approached him about the issue, Saul lied about what he'd done. Instead of rightfully accepting blame, he pointed his finger at the people.

"Yea, I have obeyed the voice of the Lord, and have gone the way which the Lord sent me, and have brought Agag the king of Amalek, and have utterly destroyed the Amalekites. But the people took of the spoil, sheep and oxen, the chief of the things which should have been utterly destroyed, to sacrifice unto the Lord thy God in Gilgal." (I Samuel 15:20-21)

Saul thought he could deceive the man of God, and ultimately God, by using the people as his scapegoat, and saying they only did it in order to offer sacrifices unto God. It's just like many of us today who feel we can do wrong and then make it up to God by giving a bigger offering during Sunday morning service, or by stopping by to visit "Mother Hester" in the hospital.

Rather than accept responsibility, we're too often unwilling to acknowledge our wrongdoing. The sad fact about it is, there will always be consequences as a result of disobedience, just like Samuel told Saul. *"Hath the Lord as great delight in burnt offerings and sacrifices as in obeying the voice of the Lord? Behold, to obey is better than sacrifice, and to hearken than the fat of rams. For rebellion is as the sin of witchcraft, and stubbornness is as iniquity and idolatry."*

In the final analysis, God will remove us from the intimate place we had with Him. As Samuel told Saul *"Because thou hast rejected the word of the Lord, he hath also rejected thee from being king".* (I Samuel 22,23)

Chapter 20: You've Got To Be Alert

When a person loses their intimate place in God, it leaves a huge spiritual void in their life. It's a dark emptiness, a cavernous hole that looms deep on the inside that somehow has to be filled. It's an ache that has to be soothed.

If you've noticed, people who backslide often go to extreme lengths to find satisfaction. They don't just settle for a little alcohol, they need the whole bottle. One woman or man just doesn't seem do it for them anymore. They need many. The reason is the void they've created from leaving God is just too big to fill.

In Saul's case, the ache came over him after Samuel informed him that he would no longer be king. It came in the form of an evil spirit God sent to torment him. The ache was so strong Saul became desperate to get it soothed. He ultimately turned to music and called in the greatest songwriter and musician of all time—the Psalmist David.

I Samuel chapter 16, verses 14 through 23 describe the power and therapeutic influence of music on man. Verse 23 sums it up. *"And it came to pass, when the evil spirit from God was upon Saul, that David took an harp, and played with his hand: so Saul was refreshed, and was well, and the evil spirit departed from him."*

This is perhaps the most clear example of the power of music on people in the Bible. It's also a classic example of the condition that exists in our world now. People who are empty, lonely, depressed, hurt or angry often turn to music to drive the evil spirits away, to soothe their aching souls, to mend their broken hearts.

"The devil, the originator of sorrowful anxieties and restless troubles, flees before the sound of music almost as much as before the Word of God....Music is a gift and grace of God, not an invention of men.
Thus it drives out the devil and makes people cheerful.
Then one forgets all wrath, impurity, and other devices." ~ Martin Luther[17]

However, while music can help relieve pain and heartbreak, satan also is using it as a weapon to do harm.

And, there's no better example of this than in the popular "hip hop" and "gansta rap" music genres. U.S. News and World Report started exposing this destructive force in an article it ran in 2001.

The late Dr. C. DeLores Tucker, a long-time politician and civil rights activist, said in the article: "the glorification of pornography, wanton disregard for civil authority, misogynistic disrespect for women and a penchant for violence are the unintended impact of hip-hop culture on today's youth. I say unintended, because hip-hop…was intended to celebrate the revival of the age-old rhymed recitations of life's problems and aspirations set to music. Unfortunately, somewhere along the way, some unscrupulous elements hijacked this influential conduit to our youth and loaded it with the evil and debasing, hate-driven messages in the lyrics we now know as gansta rap."

It caused a shiver to run down my spine when I read the June 19, 2001 music review in USA Today of the first CD produced by a group called D12. For starters, the title of the CD was "Devil's Night". What's worse, the review gave the CD three stars out of four. The lead paragraph was enough to sum up the slant of the review. It said:

"As if in acknowledgement that the 'explicit content' warning on the parental advisory sticker isn't sufficient, Eminem's Detroit rap cohorts D12 open their first album, "Devil's Night" by cautioning that you're about to hear a litany of profane and otherwise offensive terms over the next 75 minutes and if you don't like that prospect, it would be best to turn off your CD player now. . . "

The article continues that the group "spews forth one unapologetically outrageous rhyme after another about everything from deviant sex to rampant gunslinging to gleeful drug abuse. They also take their swings at gays, the media, parents and more."

Devil's Night is the title of one of the songs on the CD. Another song is titled Pistol, Pistol.

Devil's Night and Pistol, Pistol. Small wonder, so many of our young people are going over the edge and losing their lives and souls to Satan.

But the chilling influence of the "beat, beat, beat" hasn't stopped. The gangsta rap music and hip-hop music genres became so popular and lucrative, they became widely accepted by mainstream society. This has been no more apparent than the popularity of the No Limits Records label (now known as No Limits Forever Records) founded by Percy Miller or Master P, as he's known in the industry.

Chapter 20: You've Got To Be Alert

No Limits led the pack of gansta rap and hip-hop producing companies which have long line-ups of rappers who spew out lyrics that are laced with blatant use of the "N" word, vulgarity, chauvinism, demean women and portray them only as sex objects, disrespect authority figures including parents and law enforcement, promote illegal drug usage, encourage violence and glamorize gang and "thug" lifestyles in which you acquire money and gaudy symbols of success (jewelry or "bling") by any means necessary.

Studies have shown this type of music has influenced many youth the world over to attempt to emulate the gangster and thug lifestyle of the rappers. And it's evident in their defiant attitudes, postures, use of rap verbiage and tendency to want to show how much "bling" they have.

And now these genres are even influencing gospel music. Consider this quote from an article that appeared in a December 28, 2016 New York Times article "Kirk Franklin first came to crossover prominence in the mid-to-late 1990s as part of the first wave of gospel artists to take the sound and attitude of hip-hop seriously and incorporate them into their work. During that era, those worlds seemed to be miles apart. But time has a way of softening all barriers, and of late, the gospel impulse has firmly entrenched itself into hip-hop's mainstream."

The article went on to discuss how gospel artists like Franklin have now been embraced by Hip Hop artists like Kanye West and Chance the Rapper, with Franklin even appearing on albums produced by them.

But even more alarming is the conclusion drawn by gospel music producers at the Gospel Music Association meeting in May of 2015. They developed a list of 16 things they learned about the Gospel Music Industry, including "Hip-hop may just be the future of the genre, thanks to quality acts like Lecrae, KB, Andy Mineo and others, though the panelists admitted that it took years for artists to emerge from the Gospel/Christian genre that could stand toe-to-toe with their secular counterparts".

"It takes a while for that genre to find its voice," Ed Leonard, of Daywind Music Group, commented. Noting that youth groups have always been a springboard for the genre, Greg Bays, of Capital Christian Distribution Group, added, "We haven't had [new] music for youth groups in a while—hip-hop is that music."

At a time when music has captured the minds and souls of young people throughout the world, it's important that parents teach their young people to be very discriminating about what they listen to in order to avoid being negatively affected. They will sometimes need to refuse to bow to the popular genre of the time, just like Hananiah, Mishael and Azariah did. They stood up against the sound of the music Nebuchadnezzar wanted them to bow to and proved that solid upbringing could and can produce a mindset that can conquer any test, any temptation.

Bullying

Many so-called experts are now saying one primary reason for school shootings and other violent acts committed by young people is the "bullying" many less athletic or common students have to endure.

According to Psychology Today, "bullying is a distinctive pattern of harming and humiliating others, specifically those who are in some way smaller, weaker, younger or in any way more vulnerable than the bully. Bullying is not garden-variety aggression; it is a deliberate and repeated attempt to cause harm to others of lesser power. It's a very durable behavioral style, largely because bullies get what they want—at least at first. Bullies are made, not born, and it happens at an early age, if the normal aggression of 2-year-olds isn't handled well".

Bullying involves intentional, repeated hurtful acts, words or other behaviors. There is a real or perceived power imbalance between bully and victim. Psychology Today says bullying may be:

- Physical, such as punching, poking, hair pulling, beating or biting.
- Verbal, such as name-calling, teasing or gossip.
- Emotional, such as being rejected, humiliated, ostracized, having your personal characteristics berated.
- Sexual, such as harassment or actual abuse.

Being bullied is something no young person should have to deal with in our modern-day society. But despite the widespread training efforts related to respect and tolerance, bullying continues to challenge the young.

A big issue for students who may be confronted with bullying is how will they respond. The issue for parents is how do you instruct your child/

Chapter 20: You've Got To Be Alert

children to deal with a bully. Do you tell them to employ the biblical principle of "turning the other cheek" found in Matthew 5:39?

Or do you tell them what many of our parents told us: "you better stand up and fight because if you come home again after letting that kid beat you up, I'm going to give you another beating"?

I dare say not. Too many bullies are prone to pull guns now. And too many of the bullied are leveling the balance of power by taking guns to use against the bully.

Dealing with bullies and fighting is a dilemma virtually every child and every parent potentially will have to deal with at some point during the child's school years and even during their young adult lives.

Babies having babies

Another challenge young people have to deal with is teenage pregnancy. The statistics are mind boggling regarding the number of teenage girls who are getting pregnant, some as early as 10 and 12 years old.

According to statistics from the U.S. Department of Health and Human Services Office of Adolescent Health, in 2014, there were 24.2 births for every 1,000 adolescent females ages 15-19, or 249,078 babies born to females in this age group. Nearly 89 percent of these births occurred outside of marriage. The 2014 teen birth rate indicates a decline of nine percent from 2013 when the birth rate was 26.5 per 1,000.

The article noted that even though the teen birth rate had declined almost continuously over the previous 20 years, the U.S. teen birth rate was higher than that of many other developed countries, including Canada and the United Kingdom.

Parenting at any age can be challenging, but it can be particularly difficult for adolescent parents. In 2014, just over 249,000 babies were born to teen girls between the ages of 15 and 19. Childbearing during adolescence negatively affects the parents, their children, and society. Compared with their peers who delay childbearing, teen girls who have babies are:

- Less likely to finish high school;
- More likely to rely on public assistance;
- More likely to be poor as adults; and

- More likely to have children who have poorer educational, behavioral, and health outcomes over the course of their lives than do kids born to older parents.

Sexually transmitted diseases

Pregnancy is far from the only issue that emerges when teens are sexually active. There are many others, including one that not only is dangerous, it's deadly. And that's HIV (Human Immunodeficiency Virus). HIV is the virus that can lead to AIDS (Acquired Immune Deficiency Syndrome), particularly if left untreated.

According to the Centers for Disease Control and Prevention, in 2014, youth aged 13 to 24 accounted for an estimated 22 percent of all new HIV diagnoses in the United States.

- An estimated 9,731 youth aged 13 to 24 were diagnosed with HIV in 2014 in the United States.
- Eighty-one percent (7,868) of diagnoses among youth occurred in persons aged 20 to 24.
- In 2014, an estimated 1,716 youth aged 13 to 24 were diagnosed with AIDS (the last stage of HIV) representing eight percent of total AIDS diagnoses that year.

AIDS is the top killer of young adults in 64 cities. AIDS has killed more men between the ages of 25 and 44 than accidents, homicide, heart disease and cancer. Now the latest research by medical experts is saying that the AIDS virus that causes the disease may be incurable.

But HIV and AIDS aren't the only maladies that are plaguing sexually active young people. Sexually transmitted diseases (STDs) infect three million teenagers annually.

Sixty-three percent of STD cases occur among persons less than 25 years old. There are 1.3 million cases of gonorrhea every year. There are around 500,000 new cases of herpes each year in this country.

Four million cases of chlamydia occur annually, with 10 to 30 percent of the cases affecting 15 to 19 year old youths.

What is even more disturbing is that there are over 20 different and dangerous sexually transmitted diseases running rampant among the young.

Chapter 20: You've Got To Be Alert

Illiteracy

Despite the abundant opportunities that exist in our society for people to obtain a good education, illiteracy among young people, particularly in inner city and minority communities, is a huge problem in America.

Yes, we live in the information age where technology has put the knowledge of history's best thinkers at our fingertips. But statistics show that there are still thousands of people who cannot read or properly complete a job application.

You're probably wondering how the devil is using illiteracy as a tool to destroy youth. It's simple. When our youth lack the ability to read and comprehend, it can drastically hinder their ability to obtain employment and ultimately cause them frustration, anger and lead them down a negative path.

Consider the following.

According to the Department of Justice, illiteracy and crime are closely related. It says "The link between academic failure and delinquency, violence, and crime is welded to reading failure".

The stats back up this claim. According to Begin to Read, 85 percent of all juveniles who interface with the juvenile court system are functionally illiterate, and over 70 percent of inmates in America's prisons cannot read above a fourth grade level. (Huffington Post article posted 9/6/2014 and updated 12/12/2014)

Begin to Read, a division of WriteExpress Corporation, is dedicated to helping children learn to read and to increase their reading ability. According to other statistics compiled by the organization, two-thirds of students who cannot read proficiently by the end of 4th grade will end up in jail or on welfare.

And how about this:
- Sixteen to 19 year old girls at the poverty level and below, with below average skills, are six times more likely to have out-of wedlock children than their reading counterparts.

It's a fact. Illiteracy plays a significant role in giving satan an avenue to attack our youth, and the stark statistics show that he's using it well. That's why it's so important parents do all they can to help properly educate their children so they can forge positive lives for themselves.

Suicide

The last goliath I'll mention that's attacking our youth is one that's grown to immense proportions in recent years—suicide. In 2016, suicide was the second leading cause of death of people ages 15 to 24. And, it was the sixth leading cause of death among five to 14 year-olds.

Remarkably, five hundred thousand teens try killing themselves each year and 500 of them succeed. Suicide kills youth three to six times more than homicide.

According to the website Healthychildren.org, which is sponsored by the American Academy of Pediatrics, studies show that at least 90 percent of teens who kill themselves have some type of mental health problem, such as depression, anxiety, drug or alcohol abuse, or a behavior problem.

They may also have problems at school or with friends or family, or a combination of all these things. Some teens may have been victims of sexual or physical abuse. Others may be struggling with issues related to sexual identity. Usually they have had problems for some time.

Whatever the case may be, it's astounding that young people, with so much life ahead of them, are being fooled by satan to believe it's better to end their lives than find help to deal with the problems they face.

And, the devil is doubling up his efforts to take advantage of that belief, to the point where there are thousands of websites teens have access to that encourage or promote suicide. A report came out as early as 1999 noting there were more than 100,000 websites that seemed to condone suicide and forbid entry to anyone offering to dissuade users from taking their own lives.

Healthychildren.org said the studies further suggested that young people are especially vulnerable to these kinds of influences: "Individuals who access the Net (internet) are qualitatively different to other individuals. Research already indicates they are psychologically more vulnerable with higher risk taking behavior, substance abuse and depression scores over control subjects. Most are also 14 to 24, an age group with a high suicide rate and low peer support."

There is also increasing evidence that social media is now influencing suicidal behavior among young people. There are suicide chat rooms

Chapter 20: You've Got To Be Alert

where people can go to discuss methods for killing themselves. There have been several reported cases in which young people have committed suicide as a result of being bullied on social media, like Facebook.

But the kicker is that social media has been used to show actual suicide events.

Suicide—it's a modern-day goliath, but it can be beheaded if youth exercise the principle of being **A**lert to the wicked devices satan is using to destroy them.

Chapter 21

You've Got To Be Resolute

For I am persuaded, that neither death, nor life, nor angels, nor principalities, nor powers, nor things present, nor things to come, nor height, nor depth, nor any other creature, shall be able to separate us from the love of God, which is in Christ Jesus our Lord."

~ Romans 8:38-39

It may surprise you that Albert Einstein, Ludwig van Beethoven, Thomas Edison and Terry Gooding have something in common. Yeah, I know you're chuckling about how I could list my name among some of the most renowned people of all time.

It's easy, just like me, Einstein, Beethoven and Edison were all told when they were young they'd never be successful.

In fact, when Einstein was young, his parents thought he was mentally retarded. He didn't speak until he turned four and didn't read until he was seven. His grades in school were so poor that a teacher asked him to quit, saying, "Einstein, you will never amount to anything!"

Before the start of his career, Beethoven's music teacher once said of him "as a composer, he is hopeless." And during his career, he lost his hearing and yet, he managed to produce great music—a deaf man composing music!

When Edison was a boy his teacher told him he was too stupid to learn anything. And, after setting out on his own as an inventor, he tried more than 9,000 experiments before being successful.

But look at what they accomplished!

Einstein developed the **general theory of relativity**[18], the current description of gravitation in **modern physics**[19], and one of the two pillars of **modern physics**. He won the Nobel Prize in Physics and his **intellectual** achievements and originality have made the word "Einstein" synonymous with "genius"[20].

Beethoven became one of the most famous and influential composers of all time. His best-known compositions include nine symphonies[21], five piano concertos[22], one violin concerto[23], 32 piano sonatas[24], 16 string quartets[25], his great Mass[26] the *Missa solemnis*[27] and an opera[28], *Fidelio*[29].

Edison created the first successful light bulb and is considered one of the most prolific inventors in history, holding 1,093 U.S patents to his name.

No, my name will never go down in history with the likes of Einstein, Beethoven and Edison. But, like them, I am an example of how a young person can overcome the odds when they are **R**esolute.

Being **R**esolute is a cousin to **S**ingle-**M**indedness. It means being purposeful, determined and unwavering. But I like to take it a step further from the standpoint of being obsessive about accomplishing the goals you've set for yourself.

It's about setting your face like flint, refusing to let any opposition or roadblock stop you. It's persevering, or finding a way when there seems to be no way.

When I started out in college, my academic credentials were horrible, as reflected on my high school transcript. I barely graduated with a 2.0 grade point average, the bare minimum to get me into a historically black college. I didn't really focus on the academic part of high school. I went to school for sports and the social scene. I wasn't really encouraged to hit the books real hard.

I applied to one college and went there without even visiting first. There was no internet back then, so I had no clue what to expect, nor did I have anyone available to describe for me how things would be.

Needless to say, when I got to college, I had a major problem. Now that I was there, how was I going to get through? Thank God for the roommate He gave me that first year. I describe in *Looking For A Place In The Sun* how my roommate, after totally embarrassing me with his intense study habits, subsequently influenced me and showed me how to study.

Chapter 21: You've Got To Be Resolute

And even though I eventually did very well in college, I had to work extremely hard. I had to be **R**esolute. I had to resolve myself to the fact that the only way I was going to be able to make it was to attend class every day, spend an awful lot of time in the library and burn plenty of midnight oil.

One of the first things I did was teach myself how to type, so that I could turn in good-looking reports. In order to increase my vocabulary, I read incessantly and when I didn't know what a word meant I wrote it on the edge of the page, looked it up and wrote the meaning beside it.

I was so resolved to get through college that I would let nothing deter me. Yes, when I went home on breaks I partied hard and got into many things I had no business doing. But when it came time to return to school, I dropped everything and hit the road.

I saw others who surrendered to the allure of the big money that was there to be made working in the factories back then. There were many young people I knew who took on summer jobs in a factory—just like I did—but got hooked on the money and remained there rather than return to school.

But there was something deep down inside me that refused to let me give up on my evolving dream of getting a college degree. It was a resolve that I believe was imbedded there by God.

Being **R**esolute or unwavering in what you want out of life is much easier said than done. Life often throws virtually un-hittable curve balls at you. Things happen that tend to distract you or knock you off track. Tragedies occur. Heartbreaks happen. The good times don't always roll.

Einstein, Beethoven and Edison had more than their share of setbacks, but persevered through, just like I had to do to get through college.

There were times I didn't know where the tuition money would come from. . . times I was tempted to stay home and chase the money in the factories. . . and the time the administration sent us home after a horrific tornado ravaged the campus, destroying many of the buildings and killing a number of students and campus workers.

But despite the odds, Einstein, Beethoven, Edison and I made it because we were **R**esolute. We didn't yield to the temptation to give up, to cave in. We pressed on.

Today's young people have to learn how to do the same in order to have any chance at all of making it through this maze of life. They must employ the **SMART** principle of being **R**esolute. They must be able to stand firm for what they want to accomplish. They must be able to resist the temptation of going along with the crowd, of giving up when times are tough.

They must have the attitude Hanniah, Mishael and Azzariah had when they said boldly to the king after he threatened to cast them into the midst of the burning fiery furnace.

"We are not careful to answer thee in this matter. If it be so, our God whom we serve is able to deliver us from the burning fiery furnace, and he will deliver us out of thine hand, O king." (Daniel 3:16b, 17)

They were willing to die for the God they believed in; willing to make the ultimate sacrifice. That's being resolute.

But young people have to understand the devil is not their friend. He's not a fictionalized red cartoon character, nor a figment of the mind. He's real and he's ruthless.

That's why the great New Testament Apostle Paul said:

"*Put on the whole armor of God, that ye may be able to stand against the wiles of the devil. For we wrestle not against flesh and blood, but against principalities, against powers, against the rulers of the darkness of this world, against spiritual wickedness in high places.*

"*Wherefore take unto you the whole armor of God, that you may be able to withstand in the evil day, and having done all to stand. Stand therefore, having your loins girt about with truth, and having on the breastplate of righteousness; and your feet shod with the preparation of the gospel of peace;*

"*Above all, taking the shield of faith, wherewith ye shall be able to quench all the fiery darts of the wicked. And take the helmet of salvation, and the sword of the Spirit, which is the Word of God: praying always with all prayer and supplication in the Spirit. . .*" (Ephesians 6:10-18)

When young people arm themselves with that spiritual armor, they have everything they need to stand. And when they do, they can withstand satan's onslaught and conquer all the modern-day goliaths who are after their goals, dreams and their souls.

Chapter 22

You've Got To Be Tenacious

"Behold, I come quickly. Hold that fast that thou hast, that no man take thy crown."

~ Revelations 3:11

If young people are to beat the challenges of the new millennium, the last thing they've got to do in being **SMART** is be **T**enacious. The American Heritage Dictionary defines the word tenacious as "holding firmly, as to a belief; stubborn; clinging; adhesive; tending to retain; retentive".

The **SMART** principle of being tenacious means holding on to your dreams and goals and never letting go. It means holding on to the things that are most meaningful in life, such as a Christian upbringing.

One of the biggest issues young people have is the fact that they are very impressionable, which means they can be easily and readily influenced. Young people have such a strong desire to fit in, they are quick to accept a new thing, a new fad or a new way of thinking.

It's called peer pressure, and since most young people aren't independent thinkers, they often give in to it.

It's a challenge young people face beginning very early in school, but it becomes progressively more pronounced as they matriculate to middle and then high school. But it may be the most challenging when young people go to college.

I learned this well when I went to college. College campuses are filled with a multitude of mindsets. Most college campuses typically are made up of a collection of young people from all over the world. These young people come from an assortment of backgrounds. They have a variety of different views about religion and life in general.

My hometown was relatively small. Everyone I knew generally had parents who were blue collar, factory workers. People generally thought and acted the same. Everyone listened to the same type of music and dressed in similar fashion.

But when I went to college, it was a rude awakening. I was exposed to people who behaved much differently than what I was used to. They thought differently about life than the people I grew up around. They listened to jazz music. They did things I never knew existed, like follow the daily horoscope and play weegie (ouija) board.

College was simultaneously intimidating and fascinating. It presented a whole new world to me, a world that soon started me on a path to destruction that was only prevented by God coming to my rescue.

A movie that was produced by John Singleton in 1995 does a great job of illustrating the challenge impressionable young people have when they attend college. The movie, entitled *Higher Learning*, portrays a group of young people who came from different upbringings, with different views about life. But when they set foot on campus, they were faced with a myriad of views about life that was vastly different from theirs. They immediately became confused about what was right and what was wrong.

Young people typically deal with this type of issue differently based on their individual strength of character, which is largely formed from their upbringing. Those who are strong usually become the campus leaders and influence others to follow their beliefs. Those who are weaker generally end up following the strong. Unfortunately, too many of our young people are weak in character and end up following others who are stronger of character.

Singleton's movie gives a vivid description of how one young man ended up following a group of white supremacist called skinheads. In another case, it shows the struggle a young lady has regarding her sexuality and how she fell into the trap of not knowing if she was heterosexual or homosexual.

In the final analysis, all hell broke out on the college campus. The reason being that everyone was so confused about life, their stress level was raised so high it became a pressure cooker that ultimately exploded into total chaos.

The point of Singleton's movie, while focused on the challenges faced by young people entering college, can also be applied to middle- and high-

Chapter 22: You've Got To Be Tenacious

school age youth. In general, all these youths will be confronted with people from different social, economic, ethnic and religious backgrounds.

They will face a hodgepodge of beliefs that will confuse them and cause them to question the belief system their parents instilled in them at home. Most importantly, those youth who were raised in Christian homes will be challenged to hold on to what they have been taught.

In order to do so, they will have to be tenacious not only according to Webster's academic definition, but also like how a pit bull dog holds onto a victim.

I'm sure many of you have heard stories about pit bulls and their reputation for being overly-aggressive and suddenly attacking other animals or humans. Every year in America, someone is reportedly mauled or killed by an overly-aggressive pit bull.

As of the year 2016, around 700 cities in America had bans against pit bull ownership because of their dangerous reputation.

The reason is that these dogs share the blood sport heritage of "bull baiting" which was a popular sport in England during the middle ages. To participate in the sport of bull-baiting, pit bulls were trained to harass and attack bulls (like those used in bull-fighting) grab their snouts with their vise-grip jaws and pull them to the ground.

To excel at this sport, selective breeds of bulldogs and bull terriers were bred into a compact muscular dog, characterized by tremendous jaw strength. And to maximize their jaw strength, pit bulls also use what's called a "hold and shake" bite style that's designed to inflict the greatest damage possible on their victims.

Due to public outrage, bull baiting was banned in England in 1835. Bulldog breeders and owners then moved to the sport of "ratting," where a number of rats were placed into a pit and wagers were made on how many rats the dog could kill in a certain time period. To increase agility, quickness and prey-drive in the bulldog, ratters crossed the breed with terriers. Essentially, it was the sport of ratting that combined the bulldog and terrier into the modern day pit bull terrier.

But the reason people often use pit bulls as an example of tenacity is because when they clamp their jaws on a victim, they virtually have to be shot and killed before they will let go.

In fact, during a court case in Toledo, Ohio, involving the owner of a pit bull that had killed a person, the Lucas County Dog Warden showed a videotape of a tranquilized pit bull hanging from a steel cable. The dog is essentially unconscious and still does not release its grip.

That's tenacity.

It's unfortunate that pit bull dogs have been bred to be ferocious fighters that will suddenly snap and attack other animals or people—even their owners. But the determination they have to hold onto their victim is incomparable. And, it's that kind of stedfast stubbornness, young people need to have in order to prevent satan from stealing their dreams.

They have to be willing to hold on when times are hard, when they're tired, when things don't seem to be going their way.

They have to hold on when their peers are talking about them; calling them geeks or prunes or worse when they're disciplined about getting their school work done and turned in on time.

They can't worry about trying to be "cool" just to satisfy the expectations others have for them.

They have to be like a pit bull and hold on to their life's pursuits no matter what.

They have to do like the Apostle John said in the Book of Revelation 3:11 regarding the importance of God's people holding on to their faith:

". . . hold that fast which thou hast, that no man take thy crown."

Part V

. . . And That You Might Have It (Life) More Abundantly

Chapter 23

Remember NOW Thy Creator

*"I am come that they might have life
and that they might have it more abundantly."*

~ John 10:10b

So what is the smartest thing our young people can do? What is life really all about anyway? How can a child find his or her true place in the sun? How can a child escape satan's clutches and avoid being destroyed.

It's really very simple. They must not buy into the lies of the devil, adhere to and practice the principle of being SMART and above all believe and follow the unadulterated Word of God.

The wisest man of all time—Solomon—said it best in the book of Ecclesiastes chapter 12, verse 1. He said:

"Remember now thy Creator in the days of thy youth, while the evil days come not, nor the years draw nigh, when thou shalt say, I have no pleasure in them."

He reinforced those words in verses 13 and 14 of Ecclesiastes chapter 12 by adding:

"Let us hear the conclusion of the whole matter: fear God, and keep his commandments: for this is the whole duty of man. For God shall bring every work into judgement, with every secret thing, whether it be good, or whether it be evil."

That's the proven solution. Youth must recognize their purpose for living and be determined to do it. This is their duty unto God, just like it was for the four Israeli youth after they were deported from their homeland and taken to Babylon.

Daniel and his three friends were immensely blessed—even in the midst of their captivity—as a direct result of them taking a firm stand for their God Jehovah. Despite numerous efforts to change them and prevent them from worshipping their God, they never wavered.

As a result of "remembering their creator", they immediately began being blessed after their refusal to eat *"the king's meat"* and to drink *"the wine which he drank"*. That initial stand resulted in the king finding them *"ten times better than all the magicians and astrologers that were in all his realm"* (Daniel 1:20).

Their blessings grew exponentially after God gave Daniel the interpretation of a dream King Nebuchadnezzar had. Here's a summary of the story, which is recorded in the second chapter of Daniel:

After none of the king's magicians, soothsayers or sorcerers could interpret the dream, the King was so angry he issued a decree for all the wise men to be slain, including Daniel, Hananiah, Mishael and Azariah.

But Daniel, even as a teenager, was wise enough to ask the King to give him time to seek God for the interpretation. Then, after asking his buddies, Hananiah, Mishael and Azariah to pray with him, God revealed the king's dream about the various kingdoms that would rise after his.

It was an extremely dramatic moment in the lives of the Hebrew friends when Daniel entered into the king's court to interpret the dream because it would set the stage for the blessings of God to fall upon them—but also for the jealousy of the people and anger of the soothsayers to rise against them.

"Daniel answered in the presence of the king, and said, the secret which the king hath demanded cannot the wise men, the astrologers, the magicians, the soothsayers, shew unto the king;

But there is a God in heaven that revealeth secrets, and maketh known to the king Nebuchadnezzar what shall be in the latter days. The dream, and the visions of thy head upon thy bed are these." (Daniel 2:27-28)

Daniel goes on to describe the dream in verses 29 through 45. Daniel's description was so precise there was no one who could question its veracity. The king was so moved he *"fell upon his face and worshipped Daniel. . ."* (verse 46) and then *"made Daniel a great man. . . and made him ruler over the whole province of Babylon, and chief of the governors over all the wise men of Babylon"* (verse 48).

"Then Daniel requested of the king, and he set Shadrach, Mechach and Abednego over the affairs of the province of Babylon: but Daniel sat in the gate of the king." (Daniel 2:49).

Chapter 23: Remember NOW Thy Creator

During those ancient times, the gates and gateways of eastern cities held and still hold an important part, not only in the defense of the city but in the public economy. These gates were used for such special purposes as places for public deliberation, administration of justice or where there could be an audience with kings, rulers or ambassadors (Smith's Bible Dictionary).

It was a significant promotion for Daniel to be given the position of sitting at the gate, and one he could have relished under normal circumstances. But, when it comes to the enemy, even after victories, the war is still raging and you have to stay on guard.

Yes, the four Hebrew youth passed their first test with flying colors and reaped the rewards as a result. But an even tougher test loomed around the corner.

Not long after Daniel had revealed his dream, Nebuchadnezzar became lifted up in pride and decided to have an image of gold made. After completion of the image, he demanded everyone in his province to bow down and worship it every time an assortment of musical instruments were played—and if they didn't, they'd be cast into a burning fiery furnace.

It was idol worship the Hebrew boys refused to partake of despite the possible consequences. And, it wasn't long before a group of Chaldeans reported them to the king.

Most of us know the story.

Hananiah, Mishael and Azariah were detained and brought before the King. And, despite his threats to have them thrown into the fire if they continued to refuse to bow, they boldly told him they would not. They could do that because of remembering their creator and knowing the power that he had.

Imagine their fortitude that was rooted in their Godly teaching that enabled them to withstand the pressure of giving in to the king's decree. What would you have felt if you were in town when the herald cried aloud *". . . it is commanded, O people, nations and languages, that at what time ye hear the sound of the cornet, flute, harp, sackbut, psaltery, dulcimer, and all kinds of music, ye fall down and worship the golden image that Nebuchadnezzar the king hath set up: and who falleth not down and worshippeth shall the same hour be cast into the midst of a burning fiery furnace."* (Daniel 3:4-6)

Can you feel the pressure building when the trio heard their names had been reported to the king for not obeying his command? Could you have been able to stand in the face of the king when he said to the boys? *"but if ye worship not, ye shall be cast the same hour into the midst of a burning fiery furnace; and who is that God that shall deliver you out of my hands?"* (Daniel 3:15)

Wouldn't it be wonderful if the youth of today could take such a stand? Wouldn't it be great if our young people had the same kind of mindset when it comes to trusting God?

Wouldn't it make parents swell with pride if when their children's tests and temptations came they could respond like Hananiah, Mishael and Azariah did and say to the devil *"we are not careful to answer thee in this matter. If it be so, our God whom we serve is able to deliver us from the burning fiery furnace, and he will deliver us out of thine hand, O king.*

"But if not, be it known unto thee, O king, that we will not serve thy gods, nor worship the golden image which thou hast set up." (Daniel 3:17,18)

What a testimony!

Remembering God and taking the stand they did for Him caused these boys to be delivered from the fire. Yes, Nebuchadnezzar reluctantly cast them into the burning furnace, but God himself entered it with them and protected them from all harm.

It was a defining moment for these young men because it thoroughly convinced Nebuchadnezzar that the God they served was the true and living God, that there was no God like their God.

"And the princes, governors, and captains, and the king's counsellors being gathered together, saw these men, upon whose bodies the fire had no power, nor was an hair of their head singed, neither were their coats changed, nor the smell of fire had passed on them.

"Then Nebuchadnezzar spake, and said, Blessed be the God of Shadrach, Meshach and Abednego, who hath sent his angel, and delivered his servants that trusted in him, and have changed the king's word, and

yielded their bodies, that they might not serve nor worship any god, except their own God.

"Therefore I make a decree, that every people, nation, and language, which speak anything amiss against the God of Shadrach, Meshach, and Abednego, shall be cut in pieces, and their houses shall be made a dunghill: because there is no other God that can deliver after this sort.

"Then the king promoted Shadrach, Meshach and Abednego, in the province of Babylon." (Daniel 3:27-30)

The need to sometimes stand alone

When you think about it, you don't hear too many ministers or teachers talk about Hananiah, Mishael and Azariah in the same breath with Daniel. Usually, preachers preach and teachers teach about the three Hebrew boys refusing to bow down to the music, or about Daniel being thrown into the lion's den.

It's not often they talk about the fact Daniel was kidnapped out of Israel and brought to Babylon at the same time the other Hebrew boys were. There's very little talk about Daniel, Hananiah, Mishael and Azariah being friends and all of them refusing to compromise their beliefs by eating the portion of the king's meat.

But it was Daniel whom the Bible specifically pointed out *"purposed in his heart that he would not defile himself with the portion of the king's meat, nor with the wine which he drank."* (Daniel 1:8)

I believe God gave separate testimonies about Daniel and the other three prominent young Hebrews to make a couple of important points. On the one hand, He lets us know through Hananiah, Mishael and Azariah that He will often surround us with other Christians who are strong and willing to stand together for a common cause, as they stood together when thrown into the furnace of fire.

On the other hand, I believe He separates their stories to warn us that sometimes, there won't be a sister, a brother, a father, a mother or a pastor around to stand in the fire with us. There will be times when we simply have to stand by ourselves.

Standing alone is one of the most difficult things for anyone to do. It doesn't matter if you're young or old. Not many of us like to feel that we're by ourselves, that there's no one around we can call on when we're dealing with tough issues.

When hard trials or challenges confront us, we like to be able to call someone else and ask them to join us in prayer or pray for us during their prayer times. We like people to stop by our homes so we can vent our frustrations, our fears and our inhibitions.

But just like Daniel, if young people are going to make it in life, they must understand that sometimes it's just going to be them alone confronted with a challenge that could cause them to be cast into a den of hungry lions, just like the Babylonians did Daniel.

The book of Daniel doesn't tell us where Daniel was and what he was doing when Hananiah, Mishael and Azariah were ratted out for ignoring the sound of the music and not bowing down to the image King Nebuchadnezzar had set up.

It only records the report of the Chaldeans that *"there are certain Jews whom thou hast set over the affairs of the province of Babylon, Shadrach, Meshach and Abednego; these men O King, have not regarded thee: they serve not thy gods, nor worship the golden image which thou hast set up"*. (Daniel 3:12)

While we don't know specifically where Daniel was, I believe we can surmise, that wherever he was, he wasn't bowing down to the image either. We'll have to learn how he wasn't ratted out when we get to Heaven.

What we do know is that Daniel's ultimate test came after the 44-year reign of King Nebuchadnezzar ended.

As time went by, Nebuchadnezzar died and was succeeded by his son Belshazzar. Belshazzar was not like his father who had great respect for the Hebrew's God. Rather, Belshazzar was into partying, drinking and praising the gods of gold, silver, brass, iron, wood and stone (Daniel 5:1-4).

But the true God, Jehovah, was not pleased with this and gave Belshazzar a warning to make things right by showing him the fingers of a man's hand-writing on a wall.

Chapter 23: Remember NOW Thy Creator

King Belshazzar couldn't interpret the writing on the wall and it troubled him so much, his knees knocked together and he demanded that his minions find someone to interpret what it meant.

When his soothsayers, wise men and astrologers couldn't do it, Belshazzar said *"whosoever shall read this writing, and show me the interpretation thereof, shall be clothed with scarlet, and have a chain of gold about his neck, and shall be the third ruler in the kingdom."* (Daniel 5:7)

That's when the queen remembered the man of God named Daniel, who was now older and largely forgotten.

"Now the queen, by reason of the words of the king and his lords, came into the banquet house: and the queen spake and said, O king, live forever: let not thy thoughts trouble thee, nor let thy countenance be changed:

"There is a man in thy kingdom, in whom is the spirit of the holy gods; and in the days of thy father light and understanding and wisdom, like the wisdom of the gods, was found in him; whom the king Nebuchadnezzar thy father, the king, I say, thy father, made master of the magicians, astrologers, Chaldeans and soothsayers;

"Forasmuch as an excellent spirit, and knowledge, and understanding, interpreting of dreams, and showing of hard sentences, and dissolving of doubts, were found in the same Daniel, whom the king named Belteshazzar: now let Daniel be called, and he will show the interpretation." (Daniel 5:10-12)

King Belshazzar was smart enough to listen to his wife and quickly had Daniel brought before him. And, as God would have it, Daniel's reputation as a Godly man preceded him.

As Belshazzar stated: *". . . Art thou that Daniel which art of the children of the captivity of Judah, whom the king my father brought out of Jewry? I have heard of thee, that the spirit of the gods is in thee, and that light and understanding and excellent wisdom is found in thee."* (Daniel 5:13-14)

His statement couldn't have been more true because Daniel went on to interpret the dream and was rewarded greatly as a result.

"Then commanded Belshazzar, and they clothed Daniel with scarlet, and put a chain of gold about his neck, and made a proclamation

concerning him, that he should be the third ruler in the kingdom." (Daniel 5:29)

At that point, it seemed that Daniel would have it made. But satan never stops his assault on God's people. Just when it seems like things are about to go great, he launches another attack.

In the case of Daniel, Belshazzar died the same night of his promotion. And, Darius, a Median, took over the kingdom. One of the first things Darius did in his administration was to set over the kingdom one hundred and twenty princes. He then set up three presidents, including Daniel, to watch over the princes. Because of his fame and exploits, Darius preferred Daniel *"above the presidents and princes, because an excellent spirit was in him; and the king thought to set him over the whole realm."* (Daniel 6:3)

Whenever you're being considered for the highest positions of authority, you can expect someone else to be jealous of you. And jealousy will always breed contempt.

"Then the presidents and princes sought to find occasion against Daniel concerning the kingdom." (Daniel 6:4) When they couldn't find anything they could use against him concerning the kingdom, they turned their attention to finding something they could use related to his God.

"Then said these men, we shall not find any occasion against this Daniel, except we find it against him concerning the law of his God." (Daniel 6:5) They subsequently conspired to convince Darius to sign a decree forbidding prayer for 30 days; which he did to his later regret.

Even though he knew the king signed the decree, Daniel always remembered his creator. He never strayed from his regular practice of praying three times a day. *"Now when Daniel knew that the writing was signed, he went into his house; and his windows being open in his chamber toward Jerusalem, he kneeled upon his knees three times a day, and prayed, and gave thanks before his God, as he did aforetime."* (Daniel 6:10)

We all know the results of Daniel maintaining his unwavering devotion to God. He was so focused on continuing his relationship with God, he didn't even try to hide what he was doing. It resulted in his ultimate test of faith—being thrust into the den of lions.

Chapter 23: Remember NOW Thy Creator

It was a test Daniel had to face by himself. He didn't have Hananiah, Mishael and Azariah by his side to pray with him. They weren't there to hold hands together with Daniel, to face death together with him. The Bible doesn't inform us as to where these men were at the time.

All we know is that Daniel had to face this life-threatening ordeal by himself. And despite the fact that king Darius didn't really want to throw him in with the lions, he was obligated to do it based on the decree he had been tricked into signing.

But Daniel was miraculously delivered from harm's way. In his words *"God hath sent his angel to shut the lions' mouths, that they have not hurt me."* (Daniel 6:21) Consequently, Darius ordered his entire kingdom to worship Daniel's God.

"I make a decree, that in every dominion of my kingdom men tremble and fear before the God of Daniel: for he is the living God, and stedfast for ever, and his kingdom that which shall not be destroyed, and his dominion shall be even unto the end.

"He delivereth and rescueth, and he worked signs and wonders in heaven and in earth, who hath delivered Daniel from the power of the lions. So this Daniel prospered in the reign of Darius. . ." (Daniel 6:26-28)

When you stand for God, he will stand for you

When young people make a stand for God, they can rest assured that God will always stand up for them. He will always come through to shield them from blazing fire and to *"shut the mouths of the lions"*.

Young people must be determined to never leave their Godly heritage, like Daniel and his friends, because it will always pay off for them. They must be determined to always remember their creator.

Remembering God and staying with Him will always result in good things happening in the end, in spite of how difficult a trial or test may be. That's why the Bible says *"all things work together for good to them that love God, to them who are the called according to his purpose."* (Romans 8:28).

The key is that everything works together for good *"to them that love God"*. When a person turns their back on God, their action effectively negates the blessings and protection of God in their lives.

But when a person maintains a true love for God, they will keep His commandments. They will live their lives in a manner that is consistent with His Holy Word

Chapter 24

God Is Calling

"Softly and tenderly Jesus is calling..."

~ from Gospel Hymn by Will Thompson

Young people must understand that God loves them and wants them to surrender their lives to Him. He's the one who is more than able to protect them from the hand of the enemy and lead them into an abundant life on earth and on to Heaven.

Consequently, He is always calling them. He's always beckoning them to come to Him. He's always reaching out His hand.

You've heard the statement many younger people make. "I'll give my life to God later. There's too much fun I want to have right now. I ain't no old fogey (a term used to refer to older people no longer considered hip and out of touch)".

Well, God wants the young to come now while their minds are sharp and their bodies are strong, not later when their strength has diminished. And He won't turn them into frogs. He'll turn them into prophets, ministers, kings and mighty men of valor.

Listen to God's call

Are you familiar with the tradition of "dedicating" a child to the Lord several weeks after they're born. Many parents, whether they're saved or not, have practiced this tradition over the years.

The practice of dedicating or consecrating a child originated from the Biblical tradition of parents taking their children to the temple and presenting them unto the service of the Lord.

Our Savior Jesus and the Prophet Samuel are two of the most prominent Biblical examples of children being dedicated to the Lord. The book of Luke 2:22 gives the account of Mary and Joseph taking Jesus to the temple shortly after He was born in order to dedicate Him to the Lord.[30]

"And when the days of her (Mary) purification according to the law of Moses were accomplished, they (Mary and Joseph) brought him (Jesus) to Jerusalem, to present him to the Lord".

The book of 1 Samuel, chapters one through three provide details about Samuel's dedication.

Chapter 1 tells the story of Samuel's mother Hannah who was spotted one day by the prophet Eli praying before the Lord. Eli initially thought Hannah was drunk because he didn't hear what she was saying. He only saw her lips moving.

After being questioned by the priest though, Hannah explained her plight. She wasn't drunk. She was only fervently praying that God would relieve her of the taint of barrenness.

When Eli understood, he blessed her and shortly later, God granted her request for a child, which was Samuel. She was so grateful to God for blessing her, she made the decision to offer Samuel to the service of the Lord.

Chapter 2 reports that after Samuel was weaned Hannah got her husband's permission to take him to Eli. She had to remind Eli who she was.

"Oh my lord, as thy soul liveth, my lord, I am the woman that stood by thee here, praying unto the Lord. For this child I prayed; and the Lord hath given me my petition, which I asked of him: therefore also I have lent him to the Lord; as long as he liveth he shall be lent to the Lord." (1 Samuel 1:26-27)

So, in effect, what parents are doing when they bring their newborns to church to be "dedicated" is making the statement that they are offering their child back to the Lord.

When this act is done, the child doesn't know anything about it. It's the parents' responsibility to later teach that child the Biblical, Godly principles He wants them to know. What parents have to recognize is that God takes them seriously. He takes them at their word that they are in fact going to do all they can to ensure that their child lives his or her life unto God.

Chapter 24: God Is Calling

And that starts with them making sure they're properly dedicating their lives unto Him. That starts by them being the kind of example for their child that God wants them to be.

Its also important for young people to know that after they have been dedicated to God, God is going to speak to them about serving Him. When they reach a certain age or level of maturity, God is going to go beyond the teaching they received from their parents and deal directly with them, just like He did with Samuel.

It wasn't many years later, and Samuel was still a youngster, when God began speaking to him directly. The report is found in I Samuel, 3.

"And the child Samuel ministered unto the Lord before Eli. And the word of the Lord was precious in those days; there was no open vision. And it came to pass at that time, when Eli was laid down in his place and his eyes began to wax dim, that he could not see;

"And ere the lamp of God went out in the temple of the Lord, where the ark of God was, and Samuel was laid down to sleep.

"That the Lord called Samuel; and he answered, Here am I."

As the story goes, Samuel initially thought Eli was calling him and went to Eli, asking what he wanted. Eli responded that he hadn't called him. After the same thing occurred three times, Eli recognized that it was God calling Samuel and instructed him concerning what to do.

"And the Lord called Samuel again the third time. And he arose and went to Eli, and said, Here am I; for thou didst call me. And Eli perceived that the Lord had called the child. Therefore Eli said unto Samuel, Go, lie down; and it shall be, if he call thee, that thou shalt say, Speak, Lord; for they servant heareth, So Samuel went and lay down in his place.

"And the Lord came, and stood, and called as at other times, Samuel, Samuel. Then Samuel answered, speak; for thy servant heareth." (I Samuel 3:8-10)

As a result of Samuel answering the call, God went on to use him in extraordinary ways. He became the last of the judges of Israel and the first to occupy the prophetic office. He wisely directed Israel in a revival of true worship and clearly established Israel as a theocratic kingship, meaning God was their king.

Samuel was the one God used to anoint Saul king over Israel after the people demanded a human king, and he's the one whom God sent to anoint David king after God rejected Saul for his disobedience. Samuel's importance as a spiritual leader of God's people during a period of great change in Israel's history (all found in I & II Samuel) is second only to that of Moses at the time of the Exodus.

God wants to use the young

God is still calling young people today so He can use them in great ways. The key is for them to hear Him and then to act upon what He says.

However, sometimes, young people feel that God doesn't want to use them, that they're too young or aren't important enough. But God has used young people throughout history and He wants to use them now. All that's required is that they want to be used and have the right kind of heart toward God.

Take for example an obscure young lady that never is talked about. There are no sermons preached about her, no Bible studies focused on her deeds. In fact, the Bible doesn't even state what her name is. But God used her as an example that you don't have to be well-known for Him to use you.

She is referred to only as "a little maid" who had been brought out of the land of Israel into captivity in Syria. Her story is found in 2 Kings, chapter 5. It says this little maid "waited on (served) Naaman's wife".

Most of us know the story of Naaman. He was the captain of the host of the king of Syria, a great man with his master and a mighty man of valor. But despite his military exploits and the noble status he had with the king, Naaman was a leper, who'd give anything to be healed.

And he was after his encounter with the Prophet Elisha, who instructed him to go wash in Jordan seven times.

But Naaman never would have been healed if the little maid hadn't suggested to his wife that he pay a visit to the prophet of God. She said *"would God my lord were with the prophet that is in Samaria! for he would recover him of his leprosy".* (2 Kings 5:3)

This little maid, even in her youth, obviously was a devout believer in Jehovah God and His prophet Elisha. Despite being removed from her

Chapter 24: God Is Calling

homeland, Israel, she didn't forget about her God and the man He was using during that time.

She had courage enough to make the suggestion to Naaman's wife and faith enough to believe Naaman would be healed if he humbled himself and went to see the man of God, Elisha.

The passage in II Kings 5 is the only place where this little maid is mentioned in the Bible. But this one mention is significant from the standpoint of how young people who love God and the people around them can help bring about miracles.

Yes, God will even use a little maid.

God will also call and use a young person who doesn't believe they're fit—that they can't speak because they're a child. I'm sure you've heard about The Old Testament Prophet Jeremiah. That's right, when God called him, he was around 17 years old and felt his youth disqualified him from God being able to use him. But God told him, and what He's still telling young people today, *"Say not, I am a child: for thou shalt go to all that I shall send thee"*.

God advised Jeremiah that He knew who he was even before he was formed in his mother's belly; and that even before he was born, he was ordained to be a prophet.

And, as we know, God ultimately used Jeremiah as a prophet to the southern kingdom of Judah. His ministry spanned forty years. God used Jeremiah to warn Judah about its apostasy and how they needed to repent and if they didn't they would be judged for their sins. He faced extreme opposition because of his unpopular message, but God was always with him. He became one of the boldest and bravest of all the Old Testament prophets.

God wants young people today to realize that God knows them to, and has a call on their lives to perform an important mission He has exclusively for them.

The Psalmist David is one of the most prominent examples of a young person whom God used. God used him because he had the right kind of heart. God Himself even commended the kind of heart David had, stating that David was a man *". . .after mine own heart, which shall fulfill all my will."* (Acts 13:22)

The Psalmist David is perhaps the most well-known Bible character of all time, next to Jesus. People who have never set foot in a church can tell you stories about King David. Thousands if not millions of male babies have been named after David.

David first came to prominence after Saul, the first king of Israel disobeyed God. I told the story earlier about how God rejected Saul because of his disobedience and took the kingdom away from him. That's when the young herder of sheep emerged. God sent Samuel down to the house of Jesse to identify the next King of Israel. It was to be the ruddy, baby-faced lad named David, the youngest and smallest son of the eight sons of Jesse.

But just because David wasn't physically built as well as his brothers or most other soldiers for that matter, it didn't mean that he wouldn't become a mighty warrior—through the power and anointing of God that flowed through him.

And it wasn't long before he showed his future prowess by taking it upon himself to stop the giant Goliath from shaming the soldiers of Israel.

What a sight it must have been when the fair-skinned David rejected the armor of Saul, took his sling and five smooth stones and courageously marched out to combat Goliath. All eyes must have been on him as he boldly walked toward the giant, well-armed enemy. Can you imagine the hardened Israeli soldiers who were probably laughing at and mocking David as he headed toward the giant?

But David knew something about the God that he served. He knew that *"no weapon . . . formed against him would prosper"*. (Isaiah 54:17)

That's why he declared to Goliath *"thou comest to me with a sword, and with a spear, and with a shield: but I come to thee in the name of the Lord of hosts, the God of the armies of Israel, whom thou has defied"*. (I Samuel 17:45)

The rest of the story is widely known. David slew giant Goliath, whom the Israeli army had thought invincible. He got the victory over Goliath because of his heart toward God and the fact that God was with him.

Chapter 24: God Is Calling

When a young person has a heart toward God, just like David, God will use them to slay the "goliaths" in their lives, the drugs, alcohol, violence, illicit sex, suicide, illiteracy and all the other snares the devil has set for them.

All they need to do is direct their hearts toward the God of the universe who is able to do *"exceeding, abundantly above all that we can ask or think. . ."* (Ephesians 3:19).

And, God will elevate them into positions of leadership in His church and in the communities where they live. God will use them to write songs that minister to the hearts, minds and souls of His people. God will use them to share the gospel through preaching, teaching and witnessing and cause many they come into contact with to accept Jesus Christ as Lord.

Conclusion

Be About Your Father's Business

"I must work the works of him that sent me, while it is day: the night cometh, when no man can work."

~ John 9:4

The story of David's conquest of the giant Goliath and his subsequent ascension to the throne of Israel is a classic Biblical example of how God can, will and wants to use young people. But the greatest example of all time is that of Jesus.

The book of Luke tells the story. We'll let it speak for itself.

"And when he (Jesus) was 12 years old, they went up to Jerusalem after the custom of the feast. And when they had fulfilled the days, as they returned, the child Jesus tarried behind in Jerusalem; and Joseph and his mother knew not of it. But they, supposing him to have been in the company, went a day's journey; and they sought him among their kinsfolk and acquaintance.

"And when they found him not, they turned back again to Jerusalem, seeking him. And it came to pass, that after three days they found him in the temple, sitting in the midst of the doctors, both hearing them, and asking them questions.

"And all that heard him were astonished at his understanding and answers. And when they saw him, they were amazed: and his mother said unto him, son, why hast thou thus dealt with us? Behold, thy father and I have sought thee sorrowing.

"And he said unto them, 'How is it that ye sought me? Wist ye not that I must be about my Father's business?" (Luke 2:42-49)

While Mary and Joseph didn't fully understand what Jesus meant at the time, the message is very clear today. Jesus understood the importance of effectively using the time God gives us down here on planet earth to do His business.

Young people—and we all did—typically believe they're invincible. They somehow think they're going to live forever. That was the message contained in the movie *Fame* that came out in the early 1980's. Remember the theme song that said *"fame, I'm going to live forever"*.

The fact of the matter is, none of us are going to live forever on earth, just like Michael Jackson found out. Adam and Eve can be blamed for that. We're all going to die physical deaths unless we're fortunate enough to be living when the rapture (catching away) of the church occurs.

Young people must recognize—like us older ones—that life is very short, even if we live to be the age of 70, 80 or even 100. The point is, the older you get, it seems the quicker life speeds by.

Jesus completely understood that the time he had to spend on earth was going to be short. He recognized that God had given him a mission to complete and he had to get it done.

It's no different today. All of us have been charged by God to be witnesses. Some of us have acknowledged the charge. Too many have not.

Whether you have or not, the charge is permanently cemented in the Word of God. *"Go ye into all the world, and preach the gospel to every creature. He that believeth and is baptized shall be saved; but he that believeth not shall be damned."* (Mark 16:15-16)

When a young person is willing to heed the call of God, God will empower them to accomplish His will and His mission in causing people to believe in Him, just like He did with Hananiah, Mishael, Azariah and Daniel.

Yes, they might have to experience their own type of fiery furnace or den of lions, but God will always bring them out victoriously.

If young people can maintain their integrity and trust in God, great things will always happen in their lives. God will always open doors for them. He'll always give them favor with men. He'll always meet their needs, and He'll always deliver them from danger.

God will cause people to have the highest respect for them and regard for the God they serve. And He will allow them to advance in their chosen fields of profession.

Conclusion: Be About Your Father's Business

Young people who stand for God will also become the people others look to for guidance and counsel when times get tough, just like they did with Daniel.

It's interesting that after the account of Hananiah, Mishael and Azariah being protected from the fiery furnace and their subsequent promotion in the province of Babylon, there's no other mention of them in the Book of Daniel.

But as recorded, Daniel went on to become one of the most prominent of the Old Testament prophets. He experienced visitations by angels and forecast the *"time of the end"* (Daniel 12:4).

It wasn't by accident that God used Daniel in such an important and monumental way. It was because Daniel never compromised his faith in Jehovah. He never gave in, no matter what dire, life-threatening consequences he faced.

God will do the same things He did for Daniel, Hananiah, Mishael and Azariah for young people now when they are willing to commit their lives to Him. God will give them light, understanding and excellent wisdom to successfully navigate through the challenges satan will confront them with.

When they stand firm for God, God will stand more than firm for them and elevate them in His Kingdom. The results of taking a stand for God have been illustrated numerous times in the Bible and in our modern day world. The example of the four young Hebrews clearly speaks to this:

- They found *favor with God* (Daniel 1:4).
- They found *favor with men* (Daniel 1:9).
- God gave them k*nowledge, skill in all learning, wisdom, understanding* (Daniel 1:17).
- God gave them c*ommunion or fellowship with kings* (Daniel 1:19).
- God gave them *ability above others* (Daniel 1:20).
- And, God not only promoted them several times to positions of authority within a hostile, heathen kingdom, He miraculously protected from a fiery furnace and a pack of hungry lions.

Yes, just like Nebuchadnezzar went after the best and brightest Israeli youth, satan is after our precious young people today.

But if young people want to overcome the adversary of their souls and be successful in life; if they want to live lives that are rich and full, they can definitely do so. They can be like the mighty eagles, spread their wings and fly to the highest peaks of what God has to offer us on Planet earth. They can be renowned as someone with knowledge and insight that is superior to their peers. And, most important of all, when that great trumpet sounds, they can be ready to make their way to Heaven.

All they've got to do is be **SMART**.

***S**ingle-Minded.*
***A**lert.*
***R**esolute.*
***T**enacious.*

Now go get what's yours!

Notes

[1] "Magician (fantasy)" 2017 in *Wikipedia: The Free Encyclopedia*, Wikimedia Foundation Inc., viewed 12 September 2017, <https://en.wikipedia.org/wiki/Magician_(fantasy)>.

[2] "Harry Potter (character)" 2017 in *Wikipedia: The Free Encyclopedia*, Wikimedia Foundation Inc., viewed 12 September 2017, <https://en.wikipedia.org/wiki/Harry_Potter_(character)>.

[3] "Hermione Granger" 2017 in *Wikipedia: The Free Encyclopedia*, Wikimedia Foundation Inc., viewed 12 September 2017, <https://en.wikipedia.org/wiki/Hermione_Granger>.

[4] "Ron Weasley" 2017 in *Wikipedia: The Free Encyclopedia*, Wikimedia Foundation Inc., viewed 12 September 2017, <https://en.wikipedia.org/wiki/Ron_Weasley>.

[5] "Hogwarts" 2017 in *Wikipedia: The Free Encyclopedia*, Wikimedia Foundation Inc., viewed 12 September 2017, <https://en.wikipedia.org/wiki/Hogwarts>

[6] "Lord Voldemort" 2017 in *Wikipedia: The Free Encyclopedia*, Wikimedia Foundation Inc., viewed 12 September 2017, <https://en.wikipedia.org/wiki/Lord_Voldemort>.

[7] "Highest-grossing franchises and film series" 2017 in *Wikipedia: The Free Encyclopedia*, Wikimedia Foundation Inc., viewed 12 September 2017, <https://en.wikipedia.org/wiki/List_of_highest-grossing_films#Highest-grossing_franchise_and_film_series>.

[8] "List of highest-grossing films" 2017 in *Wikipedia: The Free Encyclopedia*, Wikimedia Foundation Inc., viewed 12 September 2017, <https://en.wikipedia.org/wiki/List_of_highest-grossing_films>.

[9] "Did slain Va. girl talk to her alleged killer on messaging app?" *Crimesider Staff, CBS/AP*. CBS Interactive Inc, 3 February 2016. Viewed Sept. 12, 2017. <https://www.cbsnews.com/news/did-slain-virginia-girl-nicole-lovell-talk-to-her-alleged-killer-on-messaging-app/>.

[10] "Elementary school volunteer arrested in child porn investigation" Lynh Bui and Donna St. George. The Washington Post, 8 February 2016. Viewed Sept. 12 2017. <https://www.washingtonpost.com/local/public-safety/elementary-school-volunteer-arrested-in-child-porn-investigation/2016/02/08/c7ac45d8-ce9e-11e5-b2bc-988409ee911b_story.html?postshare=3911455021784697&tid=ss_tw&utm_term=.0511abc91a5d>.

[11] "Share of teenage mobile internet users in the United States as of March 2015, by age", 2016, *Statista: The Statistics Portal*, Statista Inc., viewed 12 September 2017. <https://www.statista.com/statistics/295148/us-teen-mobile-internet-users-by-age/>.

[12] "Average daily time spent online via mobile by internet users in North America as of 1st quarter 2015, by age group (in minutes)" 2016, *Statista: The Statistics Portal*, Statista Inc., viewed 12 September 2017. <https://www.statista.com/statistics/433849/daily-time-spent-online-mobile-age-north-america/>.

[13] "Average duration of daily internet usage worldwide in 2014, by age group and device (in hours)" 2015, *Statista: The Statistics Portal,* Statista Inc., viewed 12 September 2017. <https://www.statista.com/statistics/416850/average-duration-of-internet-use-age-device/>.

[14] "Most popular social networks and apps according to teen social media users in the United States as of November 2016, based on daily usage" 2016, *Statista: The Statistics Portal,* Statista Inc., viewed 12 September 2017. <https://www.statista.com/statistics/306947/us-teens-social-media-apps-dau/>.

[15] "After 5 Months of Sales, Colorado Sees the Downside of a Legal High" *Healy, Jack, The New York Times,* The New York Times Company., 31 May 2014. Viewed 12 September 2017. <https://www.nytimes.com/2014/06/01/us/after-5-months-of-sales-colorado-sees-the-downside-of-a-legal-high.html>.

[16] "Legalization didn't unclog prosions" *The Gazette Op/Ed,* Colorado Springs Gazette, 20 March 2015. Viewed 12 September 2017. <https://gazette.com/legalization-didnt-unclog-prisons/article/1548308>.

[17] "Martin Luther" 2017, Goodreads Inc, [n.d}. Viewed Sept 12 2017. <https://www.goodreads.com/author/show/29874.Martin_Luther>.

[18] "General relativity" 2017 *Wikipedia: The Free Encyclopedia,* Wikimedia Foundation Inc., Viewed 12 September 2017. <https://en.wikipedia.org/wiki/General_relativity>.

[19] "Modern Physics" 2017 *Wikipedia: The Free Encyclopedia,* Wikimedia Foundation Inc., Viewed 12 September 2017. <https://en.wikipedia.org/wiki/Modern_physics>.

[20] "Genius" 2017 *Wikipedia: The Free Encyclopedia,* Wikimedia Foundation Inc., Viewed 12 September 2017. <https://en.wikipedia.org/wiki/Genius>.

[21] "Symphony" 2017 *Wikipedia: The Free Encyclopedia,* Wikimedia Foundation Inc., Viewed 12 September 2017. <https://en.wikipedia.org/wiki/Symphony>.

[22] "Piano concerto" 2017 *Wikipedia: The Free Encyclopedia,* Wikimedia Foundation Inc., Viewed 12 September 2017. <https://en.wikipedia.org/wiki/Piano_concerto>.

[23] "Violin concerto" 2017 *Wikipedia: The Free Encyclopedia,* Wikimedia Foundation Inc., Viewed 12 September 2017. <https://en.wikipedia.org/wiki/Violin_concerto>.

[24] "Piano sonata" 2017 *Wikipedia: The Free Encyclopedia,* Wikimedia Foundation Inc., Viewed 12 September 2017. <https://en.wikipedia.org/wiki/Piano_sonata>.

[25] "String quartet" 2017 *Wikipedia: The Free Encyclopedia,* Wikimedia Foundation Inc., Viewed 12 September 2017 <https://en.wikipedia.org/wiki/String-quartet>.

Notes

[26] "Mass (music)" 2017 *Wikipedia: The Free Encyclopedia,* Wikimedia Foundation Inc., Viewed 12 September 2017 <https://en.wikipedia.org/wiki/Mass_(music)>.

[27] "Missa solemnis (Beethoven" 2017 *Wikipedia: The Free Encyclopedia,* Wikimedia Foundation Inc., Viewed 12 September 2017 <https://en.wikipedia.org/wiki/Missa_solemnis_(Beethoven)>.

[28] "Opera" 2017 *Wikipedia: The Free Encyclopedia,* Wikimedia Foundation Inc., Viewed 12 September 2017. <https://en.wikipedia.org/wiki/Opera>.

[29] "Fidelio" 2017 *Wikipedia: The Free Encyclopedia,* Wikimedia Foundation Inc., Viewed 12 September 2017. <https://en.wikipedia.org/wiki/Fidelio>.

[30] "Luke 2:22" 2017 *Biblia: Bible Study Online,* Faithlife Corporation., Viewed 12 September 2017. <https://biblia.com/books/esv/Luke 2.22>.

www.ingramcontent.com/pod-product-compliance
Lightning Source LLC
LaVergne TN
LVHW051554070426
835507LV00021B/2567